Problem Child

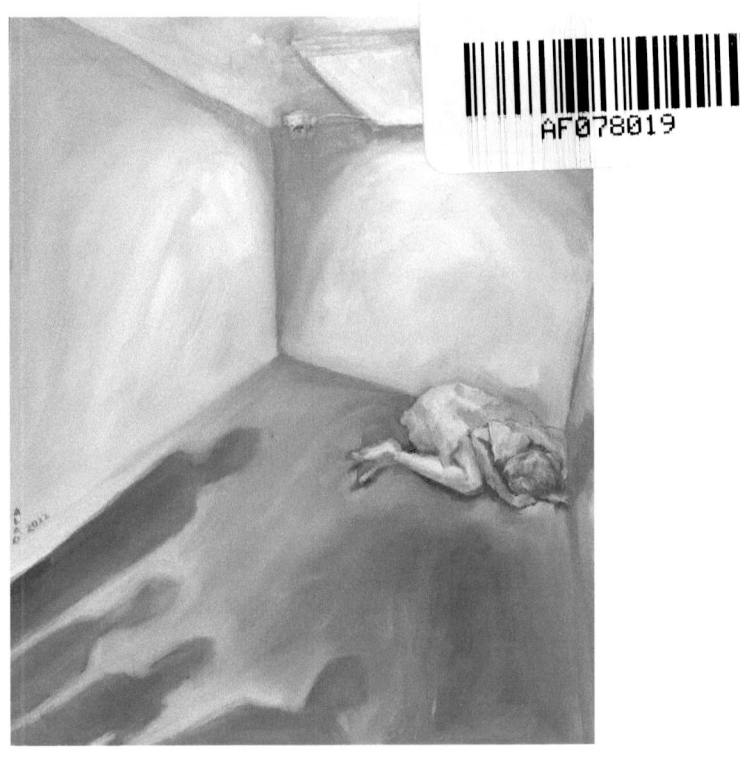

Hindsight Junior Series

Adapted from the Award-Winning Memoir
Hindsight: Coming of Age on the Streets of Hollywood

Sheryl Recinos

Copyright 2022, all rights reserved.

Ebook ISBN: 9781951542009
Paperback ISBN: 9781951542016

This book contains real stories, although some facts and names have been altered to protect the identities of people depicted in the story. All recollections are those of the author, and each person likely has their own story to tell about the events described in this book. The overall goal in sharing this story is to help young people.

No part of this book may be reproduced, or stored in a retrieval system, or transmitted in any form or by any means, electronic, mechanical, photocopying, recording, or otherwise, without express written permission of the publisher.

Cover Art: Dr. Anna Carley @bananacarley
Cover Design: Sheryl Recinos
Editor: Connie Dowell, www.bookechoes.com

Water Bear Press: Los Angeles, CA

Dedication

To Nick - Staying was probably harder. Love you.

Chapter 1
Family Meeting

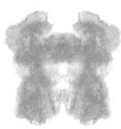

June, 1990

"Wake up!" our dad yelled up the stairs at us, again. It was a Saturday morning at the beginning of summer vacation, meant for lazy days staring at cartoons or playing video games. My older brother Nick and I were so close to beating the Legend of Zelda, and I wanted to find the Triforce once we were worthy of all three virtues: wisdom, power, and courage.

But that Saturday morning would be unlike any I had ever experienced. I wasn't going on a quest to save a princess; instead, I would start a long, harrowing journey to save myself. And I had no idea what was coming.

I raced through the motions, quickly running a wide-toothed comb through my hair and brushing my teeth. I put on my favorite t-shirt, a yellow shirt with blue hearts that had stretched until the fabric was ready to give way. It had been my older sister's shirt first, and I'd been wearing it for a few years by then.

We climbed into my dad's aging burgundy van, both my brother and I yawning but ready to get this farce of a "family meeting" over with. Our new stepmother of just six months was hospitalized in the Psych Ward. It was a place we were already familiar with, since our own mother had been there far too many times. She had a diagnosis of something called Bipolar, while our stepmom Terri was apparently Depressed. It was the reason why our dad had custody, even though most kids whose parents were divorced got to live with their moms.

There was nothing special about the drive to the hospital, no warning signs. No emergency alarm or detour. Just a regular short road trip to the place I hadn't thought much about in the past. I'd previously visited the hospital when my mom was sick, so I hadn't sensed the change that was coming.

Our dad drove down Franklin Boulevard, turned left at the mall, crossed over the interstate that led away from my small North Carolina town, coasted down New Hope Road, then turned right on Ozark Road. A tall forest mixed with pine trees and leafy, green, deciduous trees flooded both sides of the road, only interrupted by a street sign that read: Hospital Road. He followed the path up that road until a seven-story, white building came into view. I knew already that there were seven floors, because my mom had always been kept on the Seventh Floor Psych Ward when she was having a "nervous breakdown."

There wasn't anything out of place in the parking lot where we left our van. No warnings that the ground was about to shift underneath my feet. I reluctantly stood and stretched, still dreaming about that comfortable spot of carpet in front of our living room television set. Whatever they needed us to say, it needed to happen fast. We were missing a new Thundercats episode for this, and I wasn't about to miss any more of my favorite shows. He-Man and She-Ra would be over by the time we got home, and I didn't want to miss all of Saturday morning. It was the first week of summer vacation, and my brother and I had waited all week to watch our favorite shows. Today was the day we were planning to finish Zelda's quest.

We walked up the sidewalk, passing an old man waiting in a wheelchair for his ride to pick him up. The nurse standing with him looked tired, like she wanted to play video games instead, too. I didn't stop to breathe in the beautiful scent of free air. I hadn't realized how badly I would need it to fuel my lungs.

When we entered the lobby, my eyes darted to the right. The gift shop. We'd gotten candy there once, when our oldest brother David had taken us to visit Mom for something else. When she'd been admitted for something that didn't land her on the top floor. She'd needed an operation or something, and I'd been terrified that she wouldn't be okay. She had stared straight ahead, her eyes focused elsewhere as they searched the walls for bugs or whatever else she thought she saw. But I'd been there, and those white walls had been immaculately clean. Not a single speck of anything that could be mistaken for a bug.

Inside the gift shop, I could see stuffed animals, balloons, and flowers near the entrance. But instead, our dad took us straight past the information desk to the elevators. He pressed the button and an elevator arrived. We shuffled on, along with a few employees. When he tapped the button for the Seventh Floor, one of the staff members glanced in our direction. I was used to those looks already; something was wrong with my mom. But this time, we weren't here for her. We were here for my dad's new wife, the lady who hated children but married him anyway. I didn't like her at all.

The elevator passengers exited on all the normal floors as we moved upward, as we continued our ascent into the scary place. When we got to the top, my dad stepped off first.

If I had known, I wouldn't have gotten off the elevator.

I wouldn't have gotten into it to begin with.

I would've put up a fight. Maybe I would have stayed home.

Definitely, I would've found someplace to hide. Anywhere but there.

But sometimes, there's no way to predict when the world is about to implode. And there was no way to know what was about to happen to me on that seemingly ordinary Saturday morning.

Chapter 2
Psych Ward

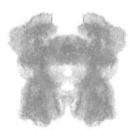

We were the last passengers on the elevator when it finally arrived on the Seventh Floor.

I had never liked Terri. My dad had introduced her to us when I was ten, in the aftermath of a hurricane that had toppled our small town in North Carolina. Hurricane Hugo. Nick had written a paper in school about a hurricane with that name, and it had hit our inland hometown with heavy winds, rain, and destruction. Hugo hadn't been as terrible as Nick's school assignment had predicted, but it had wreaked a different kind of havoc on our lives.

My mom had gone missing, for one. Something had happened to her during the storm, and we didn't realize it until several days after the rain and heavy winds had passed by. When I finally convinced my dad to drive me out to her house on the other side of town, we quickly saw the damage that the hurricane had done to her place.

The windows were shattered, and the yard was a mess. Her car was gone. I had run up the short walkway, terrified. "Mom?" I had cried out, fear filling me. I was almost ten at that time, but I already understood that something wasn't right with my mom.

Inside her house was much more chaotic. There were broken walls coated in trails of yellow and red. I wandered inside slowly, afraid to step on pieces of sharp glass. Except… there weren't any. All the glass had ended up on the outside of the house. It took me a few minutes to realize that the windows had been broken from the inside. But that meant… something worse.

I hadn't wanted to connect the dots, but the pieces fell into place. The more I studied the mess, the more I cleaned, I realized that the ruined rooms hadn't been created by a storm. My mom had destroyed everything. Every last window, dish, piece of furniture. And what had only been slightly damaged had taken on water during the continued torrential rains.

It wasn't the first time I'd seen evidence of my mom's illness, but that didn't make the dread that coursed through me any easier.

"Where is she?" I'd asked, my voice tiny and afraid.

She'd had a small house, and it didn't take long to move through each room. A terrified feeling filled the pit of my stomach, spreading out to the rest of my body. I just knew something bad had happened to my mom. I searched the two bedrooms, bathroom, kitchen, and living room. Every tiny room had been flipped over. There were crumpled papers and photographs littering the wooden floors. In my mom's bedroom, the floorboards had been smashed inward, revealing the underbelly of her small house. But she wasn't there.

We didn't find out what happened to her right away. But my dad did take us a few towns over, where he introduced us to a woman he had apparently been dating. Terri, a woman with rimmed glasses, short curly red hair, and a high-pitched Southern accent. She lived with her parents, and they had electricity and water, while our area was still without both. What was supposed to be a friendly visit to use a friend's shower became the beginning of a nightmare.

They were engaged soon after. I couldn't understand why my dad was rushing into marriage when the divorce papers from my mom had barely been signed. We had just figured out how to exist as a small family at a time when it was uncommon for dads to get custody, and he was already bringing a stranger into our home. Even worse, she was a stranger who hated kids. I couldn't figure out why she'd even wanted to marry my dad, a single dad with five kids.

"I won't go to the wedding!" I had shouted in anger, storming out of the room after he'd made his big announcement. Even my big sister Melinda had agreed, and she'd stood by my side. We were going to sit out the horrific union together.

But my dad had persisted, always worried about appearances. Always trying to put on pretenses that our home was normal. He was furious and kept ranting, "What will people think?"

I was ten at the time, and still afraid to make him mad at me, so I finally caved. But I remembered that sinking feeling as they stood at the front of her church, saying their marriage vows. What would this mean for us?

Six months later I had our answer. It would mean more Seventh Floor. We stepped off the elevator. It was a foreign world for me. My dad knew exactly where to go, though. He turned to the left, like his feet had memorized the path on so many previous visits. While we waited at a locked set of double doors, my dad pressing the buzzer for them to let us in, I twisted my head back to see what else was up here. On the opposite end of the hallway, there was an identical set of large doors, labeled Adolescent Unit.

I didn't know what that word meant yet. If I had known, I probably would've peed my pants or cried. But I certainly wouldn't have followed my dad onto the locked unit that was keeping my stepmom safe from herself. And I wouldn't have been so relaxed, chatting about video games or daydreaming about summer.

We were waiting in a large room at the beginning of the adult psych ward. Nick sat next to me at a long table. There were plastic-looking sofas at the other end of the room, along with a television against the wall. It wasn't on, which seemed like a total waste. I would've much rather been watching cartoons. Instead, we were chatting about our favorite video game and how we were going to continue our quest once we got home.

Our dad had stepped out for a moment to talk with someone. When he returned, he was with a thin man in a well-tailored suit. He had dark hair and steely eyes. His badge said Dr. Reddy, psychiatrist.

My dad was beside him, nodding in agreement with something the doctor must have said as they were entering. I'd never met a psychiatrist up close before, but my mom and my stepmom both had psychiatrists. They were special doctors who took care of people with things like bipolar disorder and depression.

Nick sat up straight, probably ready to get this over with. He was always smarter than me; he knew how to cloak his frustration with a perfect kid face. I would spend years wishing I'd figured it out as easily as he had. Sadly, my emotions were always written plain as day on my face, or at least in my eyes.

"We're here for a family meeting," Dr. Reddy said. He was

dressed up like he was going to church, but this was just a hospital.

I stared up at the man, surprised that he was playing along with the farce about my family. A stepmom was only a part of the family as long as she stayed. I didn't expect her to stay for very long, especially since she was already on the Seventh Floor. She had no reason to pretend to be mom-like. She didn't like me, and she didn't even try to hide it. And I didn't like her either.

"She's not family. She's just our stepmom." Which was technically true.

"I see," the man in an expensive suit said.

I placed an elbow on the table and let another yawn escape my throat. It was a lazy summer day, after all. And this was boring. I could've already been on my second bowl of cereal during the commercial breaks by then. Not to mention, home was much calmer with my stepmom in the hospital. I couldn't wait to get out of this place.

"Are you tired?" the psychiatrist asked.

I shrugged. "Yeah." I was eleven by then, and it was summer break. Of course, I was tired. It had been a long school year, and we had a new stepmom. I should've been home enjoying my vacation, not sitting in a hospital conference room waiting for a family meeting for this farce of a family.

The doctor smiled. "Great. We can let you rest on the other side."

I sat up straight, suddenly mimicking Nick. He had been right to be on edge. I'd been mistaken.

"What?" I asked breathlessly. What in the world was he talking about? What other side?

"I already talked to your dad. We have some beds on the other side, so that you can get some rest."

"No, thank you," I told him quickly. Suddenly I felt that feeling I had in the pit of my stomach when I found my mom's house, the one when I saw the glass on the wet grass outside each window. I turned to my dad, who had a strange look on his face. "Dad, let's go home."

He shook his head. Just then, I saw several tall men approaching the room through the glass windows lining the wall.

The men entered as I stood up. "Dad?" I asked again. He remained silent.

The men were all at least a foot taller than me. At eleven, I hadn't hit my full growth spurt yet. I was still a kid. A powerless kid.

"Let's do this the easy way," the doctor was saying, just as one of the men grabbed my arm. I yanked it back, sidestepping him. Another man reached for me, until there were several of them pinning me against the wall.

"DAD?" I called out. I couldn't see Nick beyond the wall of men in dark colored scrubs.

"We'll take good care of her," I heard the doctor saying. Tears streamed from my eyes as I tried to fight my way out of the half dozen arms that were holding me down.

"Dad, where are they taking me?" I demanded. Hot tears poured down my cheeks, and my arms hurt against the heavy adult hands that were grabbing me.

My dad didn't answer. The men pulled me away, towards the door. There was a set of double doors ahead, the same ones we had entered through just a half hour earlier. I twisted my neck around to see him, but he didn't make eye contact. Instead, he abruptly turned his head away.

The silent treatment. I'd learned that from when he was still married to my mom. They'd managed to go months without talking to each other, all while us kids maneuvered around them and tried to stay out of harm's way.

When they opened the door, I swung my arms hard and tried to escape the grasp of the men who were stealing me away from my brother. I didn't know where they were taking me. Why wouldn't they just tell me?

I wailed again. "Dad, don't do this!" I tried to break free, just as we passed the elevators. Several other men joined in, until I was being physically dragged by at least six men, all holding me at odd angles; my arms and legs were trapped, and I was a crying, screaming mess. Where were they taking me?

And why?

But my dad never answered. He stayed behind, in that room where my new stepmom's psychiatrist had asked for a family meeting. He didn't follow to make sure I was okay. He didn't chase after them and ask why they were hauling me away to some unknown place. He'd let them kidnap me, and he hadn't even intervened. He hadn't fought for me. He'd just let it happen. My dad wasn't panicking.

I was, though. I continued squirming and fighting, trying to find a way out of the grasp of these horrible men who had just stolen me.

And I didn't know if the same fate awaited my brother. Would Nick be okay? Or would they grab him, too?

The men carried me away from the row of elevators and towards the other end of the hallway. From my sideways view, I could see that sign again. Adolescent Unit. That's where they were hauling me like a captured farm animal, even as I kicked and screamed and fought. Sheer terror rolled through me. What had I done wrong? Why had my dad let them grab me? Why wasn't I allowed to go home?

Especially since just ten minutes earlier, all I had been doing was chatting with my brother about video games and Thundercats.

Chapter 3
Taken

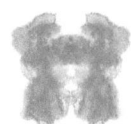

They dragged me inside, carrying me even as I fought with all my strength. These men were stealing me, and I had to get away. Maybe if I found my mom, she would help me. Or one of my older siblings. Nick hadn't been able to help; we were both too small. We were just kids. He was only a year older than me, after all. I just hoped they'd leave him alone. They already had me; that was too much.

My screams were filled with panic and rage. This was worse than a bad tv movie. "Let me go! LET ME GO!"

But they didn't. They pulled me around a corner, past a glass wall separating several nurses from their patients, and into a small room with cinder block walls. In that room, a bed was already waiting, and it had thick leather straps attached to it. The men held me down while I fought with every last bit of strength I had left. "I want my mom!"

I don't remember their words. They probably told me to be quiet or calm down. That didn't work. I had no idea what had happened, or why. What had I done to deserve this? All I did know was that they strapped me to the bed, tying down each arm and each leg. A tall woman in a nurse's uniform entered and injected the contents of a needle into my thigh.

"MOM!" I wailed. She would know what to do. If she knew my dad was letting them do this to me, she would stop them.

"Call my brother. David. Tell him," I pleaded groggily, as whatever was in that needle began to spread through my body. I felt like I was being pulled underwater,
like a heavy blanket of ocean was pushing down on top of me. "Help," I whispered before I closed my eyes.

Hours later, I squinted my eyes open. I was still in that room, a tiny room with white walls and a door at the entrance. The door was closed. A bright light shone overhead. They had left the lights on, and the room was flooded with an industrial shimmer. I stared at the door for at least ten minutes before someone opened a little square latch on it and peered in through a window.

A thick key twisted in the lock, then the door pushed inward. It was the nurse who had injected me with that poison that had made me sleepy.

"Are you going to calm down now?"

"I want my mom!" I cried, tears pouring out my eyes.

"Not this again," she grumbled.

I screamed again, at the top of my lungs. "Let me out of here! You can't do this! Call my dad! Call my mom!"

But they didn't call anyone. Instead, she scurried off, only to return with another one of those tall men in scrubs and a needle full of that sleep medicine. I tried to pull away, but I was trapped. I couldn't fight anymore since my hands and legs were locked in place, and the scary needle filled with whatever poison they were using to drug me plunged into my thigh. The fight was drained away, and I sank underwater again.

The next time I awoke, I was still alone. The windowless room was dark this time. I couldn't see, but the soreness in my arms and legs immediately reminded me where I was. I
opened my mouth to yell again. They'd made a mistake. Why was I here? Why had those men taken me? Why had my dad let them?

My throat was raw from screaming. I licked my lips, flinching at the pain as my dry tongue rolled over the cracked skin. How long had it been since they'd locked me away in this room? How long had I wasted away, screaming and fighting? My stomach growled with hunger, but I lay there, trying to devise a plan.

Fuzzy thoughts swirled through my head. The room was hot and stuffy, and my hair felt sticky. Dread coursed through my veins. That, and whatever weird meds they'd injected me with. I felt like my head was spinning and my vision was off even though I was just squinting into darkness. There were little flashes of lights in my field of vision, like fireflies fading out in a midnight sky.

If I could get them to call my dad, they would realize this was a mistake. Better yet, my mom. There was no way she'd be okay with this. She would never have let them hurt me like this.

But then, I shook my head sadly. Everything was so messed up between my parents. They'd separated when I was eight, back when I'd had my first dose of seeing what my mom's own illness looked like upfront. I couldn't remember a time when they were kind to each other, just a string of awkward family dinners with deathly silence. The only words were my dad's constant barking to finish all my peas or clean my room.

And my dad had custody. He got to decide whatever would happen to me. He'd already told me I was a "problem child" more than once. He'd told me I was going to be just
like my big brother Kevin.

A worse thought crossed my mind. Was this how it happened when they'd gotten rid of my older brother Kevin? Was that what was happening to me now? He'd been a little older, thirteen. But he'd been taken away, and he'd never come back.

Was that what was happening?

Chapter 4
Prisoner

I don't know how many times I woke up screaming, or how many times they drugged me. Hours passed. There were noises I couldn't identify outside of my cinder block cage. People talking. Sometimes, someone would peer through the glass box on the door, but it usually remained shut. Other times, it was just me, tears pouring down my cheeks. All the tears escaped my eyes until none were left. It didn't take long before my eyes ended up feeling gritty and dry, with nothing left to cry.

"I'm sorry, I'm sorry, I'm sorry!" I cried. "Whatever I did, I'm so sorry!"

No one came. "I'll be good!" I pleaded.

I eventually fell asleep again, without the help of scary needles or unknown drugs. When I woke up the next time, a different woman in a nurse's uniform was staring at me. Light filtered in from behind her, from the open doorway. She was heavyset and wore pink scrubs. Her brown bangs were curled into a poof and the rest of her hair was set in a high ponytail and crimped like she was in a band. Her badge said Trudy.

"Good morning, Sheri," she said, placing her hands on her wide hips. "Are you ready to behave?"

Behave? They stole me!

Six grown men had ripped me away from that awful "family meeting." And we'd never even seen my stepmom. Was there even a family meeting scheduled? Had it all just been a trick? Was this what my dad had wanted?

"I want..." I started. My throat was raw from all the
screaming. It hadn't done me any good. No one was coming to save me. "I want to talk to my mom."

"That's not going to happen," the woman said, placing her hands on her hips.

A tiny cough escaped my throat. Everything felt off kilter, like I was being held hostage on one of those cartoon shows. This room must be where I was supposed to be interrogated. I wondered when they were going to start pumping me with questions, only to realize they'd kidnapped the wrong person.

Trudy narrowed her eyes at me. The bright blue eye shadow on each eyelid widened, making her look even more sinister. "Are you going to start screaming again?"

I closed my eyes and thought about my choices. She'd said good morning. I'd been in this room, tied down to this bed for almost a full day. I squinted my eyes open, confirming that I was wearing a weird blue gown, which meant someone had stolen my clothes while I was sleeping and changed me. If that wasn't upsetting enough, I really needed to pee, and I was so thirsty. My throat felt dry and cracked, like I'd ripped a layer off it from screaming for my mom. And yet, she hadn't come.

"No," I decided.

"Alright. Behave for another hour and then we'll let you out."

With that, she spun around and left. The door closed behind her, and the key twisted angrily in the lock. I turned my head to the side and stared at the wall. There was no decoration. No windows at all in the room, except for the covered glass window on the door that they could open and close at their whim. No clock to tell me when an hour had passed. Without the overhead light, there was just darkness.

My screams hadn't been loud enough for the police to rush in and save me. I wondered if my mom had reported me missing yet. How would that conversation go? "Help, I think my daughter's been kidnapped. To the seventh floor. Yeah, they have an Adolescent Unit."

What was an adolescent? Was that some fancy word for a place where parents dumped their kids and let them get tortured and drugged? And why couldn't I talk to my mom? Just yesterday, I could've picked up the phone and called her whenever I wanted. She didn't have custody, but I was allowed to visit her. She even lived a few blocks away, so that I could walk over to her apartment after school if I wanted.

Tears should have been pouring down my cheeks, but even as the edges of my eyes burned, nothing came out. I was completely dry. I didn't even have tears left to cry.

I closed my eyes and tried to push back the panic that was rising in my throat. Someone had taken my clothes! That meant they'd seen me naked. And they'd given me so many injections of that weird stuff. Even after all the years they'd made me participate in DARE at school, I'd been forced to use something I didn't want. Was this one of those Stranger Danger moments that the officer had warned us about?

Breathe. Count to ten. To one hundred. Do it again. Breathe.

My heart rate sped up. My arms and legs were sore, like I'd been stretched out in this weird position for too many hours. I thought of the torture episodes on He-Man and She-Ra, when Skeletor tried to capture the good guys. Was this like that? Had the bad guys caught me, and this was their way of getting me to talk?

But life wasn't a cartoon. I wasn't a hero, and I didn't know anything important enough to be taken prisoner.

So why was I here?

I wasn't sure. I just kept trying to remind myself to breathe, not scream. To hold my words inside, even though there were bad people outside and they'd already proven they were stronger than me. Maybe if I played along with whatever they wanted, they'd let me call my mom. Wasn't that how it always worked in kidnap scenes on tv?

The hour ticked by slowly. Painfully. My bladder felt like it was going to pop, like a heavy water balloon on field day at school. My wrists and ankles ached from the heavy restraints. They were thick, brown, and completely restricted my movement. I wondered if they'd done this to my mom before. If I had any tears left, that thought would have made me cry.

When the woman finally opened the door, she came in and stood over me with a hint of reluctance on her face. Again, a tall man in scrubs accompanied her. His nametag said Jeff. Maybe Trudy and Jeff thought I was going to run.

But where would I go? My dad had left me here. It wasn't like he'd tried to stop them. Reality was starting to sink in.

He hadn't said a single word.

"Do you promise to behave?"

I nodded slowly, my eyes trained on the face of the tall man behind her. Jeff. He was one of the men who had grabbed me the previous day. *Kidnapper!* I wanted to yell. But they'd said no yelling, and I needed water. I needed to pee. I needed my clothes. I had to figure out if I was still in the same building as yesterday, and I couldn't do that while I was stuck in this torture chamber and strapped down on a bed.

I had to be smarter. So far, no one had come to save me. I might have to save myself.

But how? My mind wandered as Trudy stared me down, holding the keys to my thick leather restraints in her hands.

"Say it," Trudy commanded.

"I will… behave," I said, my voice raspy.

"Good. We'll untie you then, and I'll explain the rules after you get breakfast."

As they unlocked and removed each restraint, I felt a piece of my armor falling away. My strength was gone. I wanted to fight, to run, to flee. But I still didn't know where I was. Or where I would go.

Once my hands and legs were free, I stretched and tried to get up. Everything felt sore, like I'd fallen off a bike and mangled up my body. I moved slowly, pushing myself into a seated position. When I placed my feet on the floor, they felt cold.

Someone had stolen my socks and shoes.

I was in a blue gown that went past my knees. My back wasn't covered, and I felt a sudden chill along the naked skin on my back. I immediately reached back to hold the gown together. The bile in my stomach did a flip-flop. They drugged me and undressed me while I was sleeping. Who were these people? "I… need my clothes."

"Nope. You have to earn them," the nurse said.

Earn them? I had to get a job and buy them back? I hadn't had an allowance in years, and nobody really hired eleven-year-olds to do much of anything. I had worked the previous summer on my dad's roof for around a dollar and twenty cents an hour. I'd been terrified of heights, but Nick and I had wanted to buy some video games, so I'd conquered that fear as soon as my dad offered to pay me.

"How much will they cost?" I whispered. It was a dumb question, but I was just a kid, and I didn't understand the economy of where I had been taken.

Maybe they would let me go home to work like that again… why were my thoughts so jumbled? What had they injected me with? My thoughts rolled back to my stepmom's full medicine closet. She always looked like she was weighed down by the handful of pills she swallowed every day.

Jeff chuckled. I decided I hated him. Nothing about what had happened to me was funny.

Trudy cleared her throat, drawing my attention back to her. I forced myself to focus on the moment.

"Um… my butt is showing," I stammered, still staring at the evil man who had grabbed me. "I need to cover my underwear."

At least they'd left me with some dignity. I did still have my underwear on.

Jeff spun around and walked away, returning with another gown. It had weird snaps at the arms, and the nurse attached it over my backside like a cape. Suddenly I was double gowned with a gown over my front and one over my back. My sleeves were two layers; one from each side. I probably looked like a crazy person, but at least my butt was covered.

Gulp. Like a crazy person.

"What's an adolescent?" I needed to know.

The nurse stared down at me with pity in her eyes. "You are." I still wasn't sure what it meant, but apparently, I was an adolescent. Maybe I would have to figure it out before they would let me go home. Everything felt like a giant puzzle, like if I had been sucked into a kidnapping scene in a movie and I had to find the clues to escape.

"Oh."

"Alright, let's get you to the dayroom. Remember, you promised to behave."

I nodded. Sure, I had a lot of questions, but I would have to figure out the rules of this place. "Um, okay… but can I go to the bathroom first?"

Chapter 5
Pills

After a trip to a tiny bathroom with a door that didn't lock from the inside, I rejoined the nurse in the hallway. Surprisingly, there was a long corridor that went past the room where I'd spent the last twenty-four hours or so. There were doors on each side of the hall, and a window at the end. An old, stained carpet ran the full length from where I stood to the end of the hall.

I needed to look out the window, to confirm that I was still on the Seventh Floor. Had they moved me while I'd been sleeping? Was I still in the hospital? In my hometown, so close to my mom? Would she come rescue me? There was no way she would let my dad leave me here. I kept telling myself that because I needed to believe someone would fight for me.

"Alright, I'll show you to the dayroom."

I wrapped my arms over my chest and walked slowly behind her. My feet felt ice cold and my wrists ached from being tied down, but at least I was moving again.

The dayroom was back in the other direction, directly across from the glass wall where the nurses sat. Inside, there were three circular tables with plastic chairs around them and a sofa near another set of windows along one wall. I was in luck! I would check that window to make sure they hadn't moved me someplace secret.

There was also a door at the other end, and it had a panel of glass in the middle. I couldn't tell what was on the other side, but I needed to know.

"Alright. Get a bowl of cereal and behave," the woman told me.

I nodded, then retreated to a countertop where there were mini boxes of cereal and Styrofoam bowls. At home, we never got the cute mini boxes because they cost too much. I quickly grabbed two packs of frosted flakes, a bowl, a plastic spoon, and two cartons of milk.

Did kidnappers feed their victims? I decided that they must feed them, since they were letting me eat.

I juggled all the items between my hands and moved slowly across the room, trying not to drop anything. My stomach rumbled, reminding me how much time had passed since my last meal. They'd drugged me, starved me, and stolen my clothes. How were they able to do this, and why had my dad let them?

When I reached the table, I dumped all my loot on the top and ripped open the first box of cereal. I was beyond starving. I felt like I'd been tossed out to sea and left on a deserted island to fend for myself. Although this was worse.

A tall boy with messy hair and the scruffy beginnings of beard stubble arrived at the doorway. He paused for a moment, studying me before entering. He passed my table and went to the cereal stash, where he also grabbed two boxes of sugary cereal. I watched as he gathered his breakfast, his movements slow and methodical. He had dark, wavy hair that covered his eyes, and he was wearing a weird double gown like me. On his wrist, there was a little plastic band with tiny purple letters on it. That made me glance down at my own wrist.

There it was. A tiny plastic band with my name, date of birth, and a jumble of other numbers listed on it. That meant that I was supposed to be here.

But why?

The boy spun around and stared at me for a brief moment, as if deciding. Sit with the yelling girl or not? Slowly, he crossed the small distance and took a seat across from me.

He tore open his own cereal boxes and poured both milk cartons into the bowl, causing some of the cereal to spill over the edge. He grumbled and shoved his spoon in the bowl.

I watched him take several bites, curious. What did he know about this... hospital? Were we still on the Seventh Floor? Had he been taken from a family meeting, too?

"Hi," I said softly. Was it just me and this guy? Had someone taken him, too?

The boy looked up, his jaw moving up and down rhythmically as he chewed the cereal. He was a bit older than me, probably in high school.

He had glossy, brown eyes with dark eyebrows looming over them. I stared at him like he was an exotic creature at a zoo or something, fascinated. I wasn't alone.

He swallowed a large bite, then mumbled, "You need to eat."

I turned the box around, reading the back. There weren't any cute pictures or puzzles to solve. I always liked to read the cereal box at home, but this one wasn't fun at all.

The kidnapper nurse walked back in, the tall guy. "Sheri, hurry up and eat."

The boy's eyes widened, and worry caused his eyebrows to bend upwards. He didn't say a word, but he didn't have to. I ripped off the top of the second cardboard box and poured its contents into my bowl.

The boy was Keith, and he was fifteen. That was all I'd gotten out of him by the time he finished slurping down his sugary flakes. I, on the other hand, realized right away that my stomach was sore from pretty much everything. Yelling, crying, fighting, and their drugs. I took two bites, then had to force myself not to throw up.

Three other teens wandered into the room. They picked up cereal and milk cartons, making their way over to the other table. Nobody spoke to me, but they did look at me nervously. They all had that same jittery look about them, like they were wild-eyed victims, too.

But the strange part was how they were looking at me, like I'd done something not quite right. They seemed nervous around the adults that wandered in and out of the room, but most of their tension was pointed in my direction. I didn't understand. Wasn't it normal to fight back when a person was kidnapped? The way everyone was acting made me unsure.

They kept looking at me like I was the one who was acting wrong. But what about the men who grabbed me, or the nurse who had no problem stealing my clothes while I was sleeping?

I ran my fingers over the pale blue fabric of the weird gown set they'd put on me. It felt strange to wear something that looked like a weird dress. The gown felt itchy, like they'd used the cheapest laundry detergent on it. There were weird areas where the blue seemed too light, almost like bleach had been tossed onto it when it was waiting to be washed.

"Eat," Keith reminded me. "They'll punish you if you're defiant."

"What does that mean?" I hissed back, my voice barely above a whisper.

"Defiant? It means you don't follow directions well. A lot of us have anger issues. I mean, you sure seem to."

Anger issues? I thought back to when I was kidnapped the previous day. No, I yelled because someone stole me. I fought back because no one explained to me what was happening.

"Just eat, okay?"

I didn't understand why he kept telling me to eat, but just then, the nurse came back into the room with a small plastic tray. It looked like one of the trays they used in the elementary school cafeteria where I went to school. Except on top of it, there wasn't a weird rectangular slice of pizza or a carton of chocolate milk. Instead, there were little paper cups lined up in a row.

"Keith," she called.

The boy with the unruly hair stood, his eyes tragically hollow as he stared at nothing. He had an open milk carton in his hand. He walked across the room and took the tiny paper cup into his hand, tossed the contents into his mouth, then guzzled the milk. I watched as he automatically opened his mouth and showed the nurse that he had swallowed whatever she'd just made him take.

That uneasy feeling in the depths of my stomach grew. This was horrible. They were making these kids take meds? What if they didn't want to?

Keith tossed the empty milk carton into the trash and left the room.

"Angie."

A girl from the next table stood, let out a loud sigh, then stomped over to where Keith had just been standing. She went through the same steps; she picked up the pill cup, swallowed, and stuck out her tongue.

"Ruth."

"Felicia."

I watched both girls as they went through the motions. There was still one paper cup on the tray. Nervousness bubbled up in my stomach.

"Sheri."

Unlike the older kids, I did not immediately stand up. I did not walk across the room. I did not take those pills.

"Sheri," the lady repeated, her voice louder this time. The kidnapper, Jeff, entered the room and folded his arms over his chest.

"Come get your pills," he said.

"I don't take pills."

"Look, we're not going to argue with you. The doctor ordered pills, so you have to take them."

I didn't budge.

The nurse walked over to me with her elementary school tray and its one remaining paper cup. I stared at her, defiance building in my body. Who did she think she was? I wasn't taking whatever she had brought for me. These kids were all glossy eyed and quiet. They looked like they were halfway to zombieland.

"No."

That wasn't the answer they wanted. I felt Jeff's hand grab my arm before I could react.

"Let go of me," I cried, but he was already grabbing
me into a standing position.

Keith was staring straight ahead, trying not to look at me. The girls at the other table had their heads down, like they couldn't bear to look at me.

The paper cup had three pills in it. A small peach colored one and two white ones. I wasn't going to take them.

"I guess that wasn't enough Isolation for you."

"There's been a mistake. You need to call my dad. He'll tell you."

That made Jeff laugh, a sickening sound that gurgled out of his throat as he tugged me forward. "Your dad agreed to our treatment plan."

"Treatment?"

Treatment implied illness. That couldn't have been right. I dug in my heels, which was challenging since I'd lost my shoes. Well, they weren't lost. They'd been stolen, along with all my clothes.

"Let's go," he said, squeezing my arm as he tried to pull me forward. I took a step back but started to slip, my cold feet struggling to grip the linoleum floor.

Rage grew inside me. This man had no right to drag me around, but he was taller and stronger than me. I hadn't done anything besides refuse to take meds they shouldn't have even tried to give me.

"Call my mom. She'll fix this."

Again, the counselor laughed. "Your mom can't fix anything."

Chapter 6
Isolation

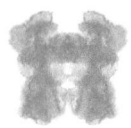

It didn't take long before I was right back in Isolation. The scary bed had been removed and it was just an empty room by the time I got locked inside again.

I protested with screams. Why were they allowed to just grab me and lock me in a room? What gave them the right to control me like this? I pushed away from both men when they'd reached for me, trying to move out of their grasp. But it didn't matter. I was a kid, and the hospital unit was locked. It wasn't like I could escape.

Both orderlies had dragged me right back to the room where I'd spent my first night. As soon as the lock clicked on the door, I felt queasy. I bellowed out the loudest scream I could manage, "Let me out!" but my throat felt like it had been sliced with glass. I'd screamed so much when they'd taken me. I'd been panicked.

That same feeling of sheer terror rose in my body again. What was happening to me? Why had they taken me? Why had my dad let them?

I pounded my fists on the door until they ached. The door wouldn't budge. The window remained closed except when a random staff member checked on me through the glass.

Tears rolled down my cheeks. Hot, salty liquid pooled at the corners of my cracked lips.

If the last twenty-four hours were any clue about how long I'd be stuck in this room again, I wasn't going to get out for a while. I finally gave up the fight, crumpling down onto the ground. I cradled my head on my knees and sobbed until there were no more tears.

Why was I here? I didn't know. The other kids had told me this was a "treatment center" for kids with problems. Kids who didn't listen to their parents, kids who were "defiant."

Defiant. They had told me that word was thrown around often. It meant that I did what I wanted, in spite of what I was told to do. But that didn't make sense.

Was I defiant for not wanting to take their drugs? I hugged my knees even tighter, feeling the oily strands of my uncombed hair moving against my legs. The gown didn't cover my legs and I felt a weird draft on the lower half of my body. I missed my clothes.

I pictured my stepmom, swallowing pills at the dining room table. She would always line them up in a little disgusting row. Green, pink, white. And then she walked around in a drugged haze, completing her household chores and incompletely cooking meals. Were the pills the reason that she never cooked chicken all the way through? Or was she just a terrible cook, oblivious to the trail of blood at the bottom of every unfinished chicken she baked?

Then, my mom's face flashed in my mind. I thought back to the trailer she'd moved into when I was eight. She'd collected me and Nick after school one day, only to drive us out to the mountains where she had announced that she was leaving our dad. But she'd stopped taking her pills, her little row of oranges and whites and whatever else she was supposed to swallow every day. And that night, the night when our heater had broken, she'd taken us to a neighbor's trailer so we could stay warm.

But something had happened. I hadn't wanted to get out of bed. When I finally awoke to her loud screams, I was scared. My mom was afraid, so I knew something bad was going on. I hadn't been willing to lift the blanket off my head until Nick had come into the room with her.

She'd taken us back to our trailer, then started to act like a rabid animal. Her movements were bizarre; her words were gibberish. My mom had then opened all the doors and turned on all the lights. She'd even set the table and thrown dollar bills all over the plates. She was talking so fast, like she didn't want to leave time to breathe in between her strings of words.

"I saw this in a movie once," she confided as she placed food haphazardly around the table. There were only three of us in the little trailer, but she had set four places with food and money.

"Mom," I had whispered, trying to get her attention. But she was someplace else, someplace far away. Even without the drugs.

My mom had bright blue eyes, even lighter in color than mine. They looked like little crystal balls, and I wished she would just tell me what was wrong. But those eyes were gazing into the night, seeing something I couldn't see. How could I have helped her? I wanted to do something, but I had only been eight at the time.

My thoughts drifted back to the way the mountain air smelled as my mom walked us away from the trailer, into the night. The air was cold, crisp.

I inhaled the air, but my nostrils took in the scent of bleach and staleness. Suddenly I sat up, remembering where I was. Isolation. White cinder block walls. White ceiling. Grey floor. White door. The floor was the only outlier. Everything was too clean, too precise.

And it reminded me of the white paint on the walls of my mom's most recent apartment. She wasn't allowed to paint them because it wasn't her property. She could hang up a few pictures, though.

Over three years had passed since that night in the mountains, and I'd become my mom's little helper. I spent as much of my free time as I could at her apartment a few blocks away from my dad's house. She was the parent I trusted. She would've never dumped me in the hospital like this. I didn't let my brain remind me of the things she had done. She was good. She was kind. She wouldn't leave me here.

But my dad... well, he had.

Although, if I really let myself ponder it for too long, I might remember what really happened after we left that trailer.

Chapter 7
Time

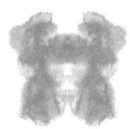

There was no clock in the Isolation room. Just the senseless passing of time in a place where I was trapped as a prisoner.

It seemed like they were checking on me through the window at regular intervals. Probably every hour. I figured it was afternoon by the time I finally heard a key unlatch the door.

"Are you ready to behave?"

I had been resting my head on my knees again. When I looked up, I recognized the man in the doorway. He was one of the orderlies who had snatched me from the dining area earlier that day. His name tag said Marvin.

"Fine," I said.

"Alright. I'll get the nurse to bring you your pills."

"I won't take pills."

He glared at me, then shook his head angrily. "Then you'll stay in here."

In here. In Isolation. Could they do that? Could they just hold me hostage like this?

I mulled over the new word Keith had taught me that morning. Defiant. Refusing to do things that adults told me to do. But was there another word, a more appropriate word? Why did I have to do whatever they said if what they wanted me to do didn't even make sense? Besides, my "doctor" hadn't even talked with me after letting them lock me up. All he'd done was capture me and drug me so far.

"Do I at least get lunch?" I asked. My stomach had finally settled down, and it was mostly empty.

"I'll see if we have anything left."

With that, he closed the door and left.

The key twisted in the lock, reminding me that I wasn't free.

There was nothing I could do but wait. I wanted to jump up and bang on the door again or scream again. But I was tired and hungry. The drugged sleep I'd had the night before hadn't made me feel like I'd rested. Instead, I was on edge. And I didn't want them to tie me up again. My wrists were still sore from the restraints.

How was I supposed to get out of there? I thought back to the roomful of teens at breakfast. Keith, the kid who told me to eat and had whispered a few things to me about the program. The teens who had walked up to the nurse in a drugged haze, willing to take their pills without defiantly refusing them.

As I sat there, not knowing whether or not I'd get fed or get released, I thought about the most bizarre kidnapper plots I'd seen on tv over the years. But hadn't the kids this morning convinced me that I hadn't been kidnapped? The presence of other kids meant that this was a place for kids. That this was punishment… for being "defiant?"

I thought about home. About the arguments I'd had lately with my dad and my stepmom Terri. I hadn't wanted to eat her food, and he'd constantly told me I was offending her. But it was gross, and my stomach always hurt after I ate it. My dad hadn't cared, even when I'd begged for permission to just eat a sandwich. Was I supposed to just eat whatever she slopped in front of us?

Before my dad had married her just six months earlier, we'd settled into a routine. I would walk to the library after school, then get home before he did at 5:30 each night. I had free time to read a few of my favorite books, mostly The Babysitter's Club or some cool science book. I usually sat at one of the fluffy chairs by the window, immersed in a book, until it started to get darker outside. Then, I walked or ran as quickly as I could so I could make it home first.

We'd even had a few decent moments. He'd taken me and Nick on a few bike rides, and we'd gone as far as a bridge across town. He'd done fatherly things like pack apples and drinks. We'd had fun.

So, it didn't make sense. Sure, I'd been mean to my stepmom. But I was no expert on how to treat a stepparent. There hadn't been instruction manuals. And she didn't like kids AT ALL. She'd been all too proud to tell me more than once that she didn't want kids. And she'd married my dad, a guy with five kids. It didn't make any sense. None of us liked her. Melinda and I had refused to go to the wedding. We'd only agreed to go when our dad pleaded with us. "What will people think?" he'd asked over and over again. We'd attended, just to get him to leave us alone. And even my older brother David joked with me about my stepmom, whispering our nickname for her behind her back when no one else could hear. "Terri the Terror." Nick was the only one who mostly kept his mouth shut. If Kevin had been around, he would've surely sided with me. But he'd been sent away, too.

I didn't like to keep my room clean. Was that why I was there? I thought about the stuffed animals that hadn't made it back into the toybox, or the clothes I hadn't hung up after I'd washed them. My shoes that were tossed wherever they landed in my room. But it wasn't that awful, was it? I'd cleaned my mom's house after Hurricane Hugo. My mom's house had been literally destroyed. The windows had been smashed. She'd punched them out in a manic rage, then the torrential rain from the hurricane had gotten inside. All her photos and documents had been thrown all over the place, either by her or by the wind. Everything was soaked. I was the one who had begged to salvage everything, and I'd gone there every afternoon until I'd boxed up all her belongings and laid out all her photos on towels in our basement. I'd dried her memories in hopes that I could save them. I knew what filth looked like; I knew the difference between a condemned house and a messy room.

My dad and I fought about stupid things, like whether or not I'd wear socks. I'd accidentally skipped wearing them one day, and he'd chewed me out the whole way to school. So maybe I'd continued to not wear them after that. I was rebelling in stupid little ways, but did that mean I was defiant?

The most I could come up with was when I'd skipped school earlier in the year. I hadn't even realized how often I'd been skipping, at least, not until my fifth-grade teacher had pulled me out in the hallway and told me off. She'd let me know that she'd been paying attention to my absences, and that if I missed the next day for a mid-week "vacation," she'd call the county truancy officer to go pick me up. I'd stopped pretending I was sick after my stepmom had moved in, anyway, so I hadn't even ditched class for almost six months. And when I had, all I'd done was watch tv or play video games. It wasn't like I was smoking or doing drugs. I was a boring kid who liked to fake stomachaches and knew how to make a thermometer just hot enough to pretend I had a fever. The trick was to also use a warm cloth to make my forehead a little bit hot. But that was old news.

I just wasn't sure what I'd done that was so wrong. Why was I locked in Isolation, when all my classmates got to spend their summertime relaxing? When my own brother was probably beating Zelda without me?

I couldn't figure out why my dad was so mad at me. Did he hate me? He and my mom had kicked Kevin out when he was thirteen, sending him off to foster care. Was that his plan for me?

After all, he'd always grumbled that he only wanted four kids. And he had a habit of saying I was just like Kevin. Well, if Kevin was a kid who just liked to read books at the library, didn't put his toys away, sometimes skipped school, and didn't like socks, then maybe I was. But how could I know? He'd been gone since I was five. I didn't know who he was, let alone where he was.

Chapter 8
Fighting with Nick

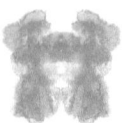

At the next window check, the door was unlatched once again. A different orderly set down a plastic tray that had a carton of milk and a sandwich wrapped in plastic. Without even speaking to me, the man closed and relocked the door.

As if I was an inmate somewhere, and I was dangerous. I shivered from my spot against the wall. What had my dad told them about me? I wasn't a fighter. Well, except when I was fighting my brother. But that was normal, right?

Maybe that was it. I didn't move towards the food, just leaned my head back against the wall and thought about the times Nick and I had fought over the years. We'd had some rough battles. He'd had his growth spurt first and had lorded over me.

We'd fought with fists and open palms. Punches and slaps. After Karate Kid came out, we'd pretended we knew kicks and karate chops. But we were untrained and angry.

After our parents had separated, our fighting had escalated. And I'd grown taller, so I was almost even with Nick. I remembered one day at school when I'd stepped near the soccer field to ask him what time our mom was picking us up.

"Go away!" he'd shouted.

"Is she coming here or meeting us at the house?" I persisted. I wanted to know. Were we taking the bus home? Were we walking? Was our mom picking us up? I wasn't
sure.

He stormed right up to me and kicked me in my shin, hard. With soccer cleats. So, I did the thing that embarrassed little sisters do. I marched around the walking path that surrounded the soccer field, searching for the perfect rock. It was oval, heavy, and fit in my palm. I polished it all the way around the field, until I was right back in the spot where he'd kicked me.

That's when I threw it at him. He screamed, surprised. And there was blood. I'd managed to hit him square in the head.

"Both of you, principal's office, NOW!" one of the teachers scolded.

We wrestled a bit on the way to the office. I was in fourth or fifth grade, and by the time we got to the office, my shirt was torn, and I had dirt on my arms and face. Nick didn't look much better.

The principal stared at both of us in disbelief. "Enough!" he told us. "You have got to keep your fighting at home."

That was his answer. That, and he paddled us. It was the standard punishment in North Carolina schools at the time. I didn't even question it.

I let out a sigh. Maybe I was a brat. Maybe I was defiant. But I wasn't the only one. So why had my dad chosen to leave me here and not Nick?

I added the fighting to my list. We'd fought a lot, but that took two people. But maybe that was enough, since I was the younger kid, and my dad didn't listen to a word I said. Maybe all the little things were enough to declare me a Problem Child once and for all. My dad had been throwing hints at me like daggers for the past six months. Ever since my stepmom had moved in.

I was an inconvenience to her. Before she'd moved in, I'd helped out with cooking and cleaning. But now that she was there, I wasn't allowed to cook, and my cleaning techniques weren't "Southern" enough. Another reminder that my family had been born up North and we'd never quite fit in down there. Or maybe it was just me. Even my wicked stepmother had decided I didn't belong there.

Was that it? Had Terri asked for my dad to send me away?

Probably, I realized. I'd refused to go to the wedding and had only relented after a lot of coaxing. I'd stood up to her when she'd told me I was too loud, too fat, too messy. She'd criticized everything about me since the day she'd moved in.

And I made her "more depressed" when I refused to eat her food.

Maybe I really was as bad as my dad must have said. Maybe I was the problem. Because from where I sat in the little, white room, I was the only member of my family in complete, utter Isolation.

Chapter 9
Forced Meds

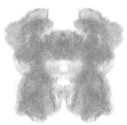

Hours passed. Eventually I caved and ate part of the sandwich. It had mayonnaise on it, though. My stomach had never been able to tolerate mayonnaise, so I sat against the wall holding my hand over my gurgling belly. I felt like I was going to be sick.

At least four more window checks happened before the door was unlocked again. The person who opened the door was someone I hadn't met yet.

She was tall, had short, brown hair, and her eyes were illuminated by bright blue eye shadow. Still living in the 80s, even though it was finally 1990. Veronica, according to her name tag.

"So what's it gonna be, Sheri?" the woman asked.

I shrugged. "How long can they keep me here?"

"As long as it takes."

I thought about that. They did have the keys, and apparently, they had my dad's permission. They could do whatever they wanted to me. In fact, they already had. They'd forgotten to send dinner; they'd kidnapped me the previous day; they'd roughhoused me that morning. They were adults and they were in charge. That was the first thing they'd shown me.

"I need to go to the bathroom."

"You need to take the pills first."

What? But I had to pee!

"Don't I have rights?"

"No. You're a kid. You have to do what we say."

I wanted to scream; in fact, I had screamed already. A lot. And look where that had gotten me? I wanted to cry, but there were no tears left. What use was it? They could leave me in that little room, alone. Forever.

Is this what had happened to my mom all the times she'd been sent away to the hospital? That thought alone sent a shockwave of fear through my body. Was this why she was always so... distant?

"Fine," I mumbled.

"Fine, you'll take them?"

"Whatever," I said.

The woman left again, only to return a few minutes later with a tiny paper cup that had two pills in it.

"What are they?"

I could tell my questions were bothering her because she scowled at me. "Are you going to take them or not?"

"Can't I at least ask what I'm supposed to take?"

"Lithium and Depakote."

I stared at the two pills. Peach and white colored. I had heard of Lithium; my mom was on it and had told me once that it made her hands shake. I thought about the way they always trembled, even when she rested them on the table. I'd never heard of Depakote.

"And then you'll let me go to the bathroom?"

"After you take them."

I held out my hand and let the woman dump both pills into my palm. She passed me a tiny cup of water. I drank as little as I could get away with to push the unwanted pills down my throat, since my bladder was so full that my stomach hurt. "Okay," I said, starting to stand up.

"Wait here for thirty minutes first."

I leaned back against the wall, bracing myself. "What?" I cried out. "Why? I have to pee. You said I could go."

"Not for thirty minutes. I can't let you vomit out those pills."

Vomit pills? I'd never heard of anything like that. But I figured that was one way to get them out if it came down to it. At least the evil woman was teaching me a few tricks along with being a liar.

"You said I could go. I really, really need to pee."

"I'll bring you a vomit basin, then."

"But..." She had lied. She had really lied to me! That was when I realized that there was absolutely nothing that I could do about it. Nobody was looking out for me. Nobody would protect me. I already had bruises all over my arms and legs from being ied to the bed and forcibly moved into Isolation more than once. These people were in control, not me.

She folded her arms over her chest. "Do you need to go or not?"

I nodded slowly, the shock rolling its way through me. They had stolen everything from me. My freedom. My rights. And now I would have to pee into a plastic container.

"Fine. But please bring toilet paper, too."

Veronica the nurse did bring me a hideous pink container and a few sheets of paper, but I wouldn't forgive her for lying to me. I peed in the bucket because I had to, since they'd all decided to treat me like a caged animal. Even after I'd caved in and taken their stupid pills.

It wasn't fair. Nothing about this place was fair.

And it didn't seem like anyone cared.

Chapter 10
Pregnant Roommate

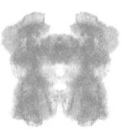

My new room was a strange hospital room with two beds in it. Both beds were set apart from each other, their fake wooden headboards against opposite walls. They had a strange institutional appearance, both made up with plain white sheets that mirrored the walls and ceiling.

Nothing about this place made sense to me. My room smelled the way I expected a hospital room to smell, but it didn't have any of the cheer I'd seen when I'd visited my mom in a regular room downstairs the previous year, back when something medical was wrong with her. Something... not mental.

The further side of the room looked emptier; the one closest to the dayroom had a few personal items atop a small, wooden table at the bedside. There was a pad of paper and a birthday card.

I swallowed hard. I wouldn't have wanted to spend a birthday here. But the pad of paper made me think of my pen pals. If only I could hop on a plane or boat and escape to New Zealand, that faraway place where my Thundercats pen pal Roxanne lived. I imagined her dad wouldn't send her to a place like this.

My hands clenched into little fists by my sides. I wanted out. I wanted to be home, sitting in my slightly messy room, thumbing through my Thundercats comic books, dreaming of living in one of the exotic places in the back of the book.

Kids from all over the world sent in letters asking for pen pals, and I had made three friends from the pen pal club. Roxanne, a boy from Canada named David, and a girl in Connecticut named Ruby. I wondered for the first time about their families.

Pen pals said things like "I have two brothers and live with my mom and dad." But they never said, "I have divorced parents, and my mom is bipolar, and my stepmom is depressed, and they sent one of my brothers to foster care because he behaved badly, but oh, by the way, he was adopted, and they changed their minds."

I wanted out. But for the first time, I wondered if I even wanted to go back. How could I, after what my dad had done?

Veronica pointed to the empty side of the room, as if I hadn't already figured out which bed was mine. "Okay," I told her, wandering over to the undecorated bed. She propped the door open as she left. Apparently, closed doors were not allowed around here.

I let out a long, sad sigh. I'd cried too much over the last thirty-six hours or so. It was already my second night away from home, and I doubted I had any tears left inside me, and it didn't matter anyway. I'd spent most of my first two days in Isolation and I'd only been offered a bowl of cereal and a mayonnaise-laden sandwich during that time. I'd barely had anything to drink. My stomach rumbled. These monsters were in control of everything.

But what exactly was I supposed to do?

On my mysterious roommate's side of the room, there was a window. On my side, there was a door. I figured that was the bathroom. I headed over to the window and peered down.

We really were at the top. Seventh Floor. Nowhere to escape.

Still, I stretched out my arms and fiddled with the edges of the window. Everything was bolted down pretty tight. But if I could find a loose window, maybe I could fashion one of those sheet ropes that I'd seen in cartoons my whole life. I spun around, studying the sheets again. They were pretty thin, but I was just eleven so maybe they'd hold my weight. Maybe.

I glanced back down. The view from my room was the back entrance of the hospital. There was a loading dock and some solid looking cement.

I cringed. If I wasn't careful, I could really get hurt from that big of a fall.

"I'm Irene," a voice said from the doorway. "You're the yeller, right?"

I spun around, expecting to see someone that had been in the dayroom earlier. Instead, I saw a girl I hadn't met yet. She was a little older, had wavy, dark hair, and her belly was huge.

"Are you...?" I asked, my voice trailing off.

"Yup. Pregnant."

I folded my arms over my chest, suddenly feeling too small to be here.

"You have a name?"

"Sheri."

"Well, Sheri," she said, "You're on my side of the room."

I nodded, backing away from her window slowly. "Sorry," I told her, moving over to my empty part of the room. The white sheets looked freshly bleached, and the room seemed… sterile.

My head was spinning. I wasn't sure if it was from not sleeping or from the medicine that was now dissolving in my stomach or from being grabbed by those men. Maybe a little of everything. I plopped down on my bed, still staring at her enormous belly. I hadn't had sex education yet. That class was supposed to happen in sixth grade, but I wouldn't start sixth grade until summer ended. And only if they let me out of this place.

"Are you… married?" I asked.

The girl laughed. "I'm sixteen," she replied, as if that answered my question.

"I just turned eleven," I said. Only two months earlier, actually.

She raised her eyebrows. "Wow," she said. "Eleven. That's… young."

I shrugged. "Yeah. I don't think I'm supposed to be here."

Irene placed a hand on her belly and seemed to think it over for a moment. "You and me both, little one. You and me both."

Chapter 11
Escape Plan

When it was my turn to take a shower that night, I turned the water on and picked at grout in the shower. If I removed the tiles on the wall, would I be able to crawl downwards? Was there a shaft between the walls that would get me down to the first floor? I imagined scaling a huge metal structure, like a large playground, and moving myself towards an awaiting exit. One shaky step at a time. Just like the movies, right?

I managed to break a little piece of grout off from the wall, then frantically rubbed my fingernails along the little blue and red tiles. Maybe I should have marveled at the fact that this room wasn't an unhealthy white color, but instead, I was too busy trying to disassemble everything.

My thumbnail split open, and I gasped. Blood poured out of it. A sudden pain gnawed its way up my fingers. Crap. I stood up and tried to rinse it with water, but it continued to trickle red. Next, I clamped a finger right under where it was bleeding, applying pressure until it stopped. At least I'd learned a few things, since I didn't have a mom at home to help me when I got hurt. I managed to make the bleeding stop, but my finger stung when I got soap on it.

I double and triple checked the tiles. Nothing looked out of place. No one would be able to detect my weird escape plan.

So much for showering, I realized. I rinsed myself mostly with water and quickly changed back into my weird two-gown dress. The faded, light blue cloth felt weird and itched against my skin. I wasn't a dress-wearer, and without shorts or pants, I felt exposed.

When I got out of the shower, Irene raised an eyebrow in my direction, but didn't ask. Had she heard me trying to dig my way out?

While Irene took her turn in the bathroom, I sat down on the floor near the doorway, just far enough out of view that the nurses wouldn't see me. We were at the last room on the long hallway, but there didn't seem to be any escape routes.

I studied the ceiling tiles in the hallway. They were different than the ones in my room; they were made up of weird, white and grey squares, almost like a checkerboard. They looked like the kind of tiles that could be pushed upward. They were the same all the way down the hall, and probably outside of it. I wondered how I would get up there into the ceiling, and if I could crawl all the way off the Adolescent Unit to safety.

I didn't want to try to figure out where I would go next. It would be a long walk to my mom's house, and I figured my dad would look for me there anyway. I needed to do more than just escape. I needed to find a new life. New parents. People that didn't just abandon me in the hospital without a warning. A parent that didn't allow grown men to hurt me.

"You're just going to get in more trouble if they find you sitting there," Irene said from behind me.

I turned around and saw my very pregnant roommate, her faded blue gown stretched to cover her belly. Her hair was dripping wet from the shower, and she was running a towel through the ends of her curls.

She seemed to know a lot more than me, and I really was tired of that Isolation room. I took one more wistful glance up at the tiles as I stood, then paused in place. My legs didn't feel connected to my body.

"Do they make you take meds, too?" I whispered.

Irene sighed. "Yes and no. I'm pregnant, so they can't give me too many. Are you feeling okay?"

I shook my head slowly, realizing my vision was blurrier than usual. "No. My legs feel wobbly, and my stomach hurts."

"Do you want some crackers?" she offered, showing me her secret stash in a bag near her bed.

I nodded slowly. "Yeah. I'm so hungry."

She met me in the doorway and looped an arm through mine, then walked me to my bed. I decided Irene would be a good mom, because she took care of me that first night I had to stay in an actual hospital room. I wasn't going to count the previous night because that was… horrible.

Chapter 12
Failed Escape

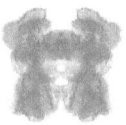

As I closed my eyes and tried to force myself to sleep that night, I thought about the only time I'd tried to leave before. It had been dark, and the night sky had only been illuminated by the distant lights of the nearby shopping center.

I'd been so young. Five years old. I didn't have much of a plan, just a childish notion that if I showed up at the corner drugstore by my house, maybe somebody would agree to be my new parents.

When I slipped out of the house and closed the door behind me, I was sure I'd been quiet. I tiptoed across the side yard towards the fence that separated my dad's yard from the bank's property next door.

Because we lived at the edge of a neighborhood that spilled into a shopping center, there was always an overly bright light shining right near the line of our fence. I could see it trickling through the row of trees that my dad had planted along the side of our yard.

There was an area that wasn't fenced, near the front of our property. If I could just make it across the lawn and over to the other side, maybe I'd find my way into a new life.

My older brother Kevin had been sent away to foster care the previous week. Why had my parents gotten rid of one of their kids? More importantly, was I next?

I didn't want to stick around and find out. It wasn't like I understood anything about my family back then. I just knew that something wasn't right. Something was, in fact, very, very wrong.

I stepped onto the driveway, a river blocking me from my destination. My tiny feet stepped on gravel, letting out a telltale crunch.

Behind me, the door snapped open, and a light shone across the yard.

"Who's out there?"

It was my dad. He sounded angry.

A ray of light moved carefully across the yard. His flashlight.

I stood perfectly still, hoping that I wouldn't be detected. All I had to do was make it across the yard, to the fence line. I was so close!

But then, the light landed on me.

"What are you doing?" my dad shouted. He saw me. Tiny, five-year-old me, hovering in the driveway like I was surrounded by lava. Wearing a backpack.

He would know. He was a smart man; he'd figure it out.

When I turned around, I saw him standing at the doorway. He hadn't even left his spot. David was beside him, holding a baseball bat. They were ready to take down an intruder, but nobody had been trying to break in.

No. I'd been trying to break out.

"Go inside," my dad scolded me.

I wished I'd had the courage to take off running. To escape anyway. Maybe someone would've found me. Taken me in. Given me a new life.

But I went inside. It's not like I had a million options. At five, I wasn't supposed to be awake that late, let alone walking in the middle of the night to anywhere else.

"We'll talk about this in the morning," my dad had said. But we didn't talk about it. We were a family that pretended bad things didn't happen, even if they fueled forest fires that would rage onward for years.

I opened my eyes, giving up the childish hope of sleeping through the night. The hallway light shone into the room, reminding me that there was always someone watching. There was always a person between me and safety.

And even though I hadn't thought about it since I was five, suddenly the only thing I wanted was to figure out how to escape.

Chapter 13
Group Therapy

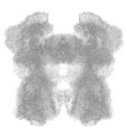

A half dozen other "adolescents" sat around me. I had learned that adolescent was a broad term that covered all our ages, from my young age of eleven years old to the pregnant girl, who was sixteen already. It felt like a sticky word meant to capture younger kids. Problem children. Me.

We were seated in a circle and two of the staff members sat across from each other. They each held their own clipboard, where they took notes while each person spoke. I sat all the way back in my chair, so far back that my feet didn't touch the floor. I dangled my little kid feet just above the linoleum and glanced nervously around the room.

"Miriam, how was your visit with your parents?" the man across from me asked. He was wearing a dark green sweater that reminded me of a soap commercial.

The girl who he was speaking with, Miriam, pulled her legs against her chest and let out a sigh. In a high-pitched voice, she told the prying man, "The same."

"Let's explore that," he continued. "How did you feel when your mom said you weren't ready to come home yet?"

Miriam's shoulders tugged upwards, then dropped back down again in a sudden motion. Her dark hair was pulled back in a tight braid, but the edges were coming undone with each movement. "I don't know. Angry. Sad," she said. "You know, the same. She doesn't want me to come home. I'm used to it."

I thought about my dad. Was that what had happened? Had he finally decided that he didn't want me at home, either? After all, he'd sent one of my brothers off to foster care when he was only thirteen. I'd been five at the time, so I hadn't really understood it. All I knew was that one day Kevin was gone. A few weeks later, my parents had replaced him with a loud foreign exchange student from Germany, Martin. They didn't keep that kid around for very long, either.

I leaned back a little more, tilting my head back so I could see the ceiling. There were tiles above us, and I dreamt of grabbing a tall chair or ladder and escaping through the roof. I'd already confirmed that the hallway outside had the same tiles. Maybe if I crawled?

But where would I go?

"I see," the man said, then decided to focus on me. "Alright, Sheri. You're new here. Can you tell us why you're here?"

My cheeks felt warm as everyone turned to look at me. Well, half of them. Some of them were zoning out, too drugged up to care. I was feeling a bit fuzzy, too. They'd made me take more pills at breakfast. I might not make it up a ladder without toppling over.

My thoughts were all over the place. I didn't like feeling that way. Not at all.

"I don't know," I mumbled.

"Of course you do," the man told me. He waited.

I stared at him. "Those men grabbed me and forced me to come here. All I was doing was waiting for a family conference."

"Right. With your..." he glanced down at his clipboard, "stepmom?"

I shrugged. "Yeah."

"Alright. And it says here that your mom has bipolar?"

He had no right to say that in front of everyone! I opened my mouth to tell him to stop, but he continued. I glanced away, staring at the door at the far side of the room. My vision split in two and there were two doors all of a sudden. I squeezed my eyes shut, and when I reopened them, there was only one door.

"And the doc says you're bipolar, too."

"No, I'm not," I said adamantly. My mom's face flashed across my mind, a picture that reminded me what that diagnosis meant. Her wild eyes, staring past me and Nick back on the mountain before she left us by the side of the road in the middle of the night. The way she rambled on and didn't make sense. The things she'd said before she'd taken us on that long walk to the middle of nowhere...

She was nuts. She was the one who had done crazy things, and I wasn't anything like her. I refused to believe that a doctor who had not come to see me since locking me up in this place had decided I was just like her.

I lowered my feet back to the floor, pressing them firmly into the linoleum. At least I had socks, finally. My feet didn't feel like ice against the cold ground. "How could he say such a thing? He hasn't even talked to me!"

The counselor shrugged. "He's the doc."

"I'm done."

I stood up abruptly and walked straight across the room, wrapping my hand on the doorknob of the awaiting door. It didn't budge. I was still locked in.

A sizable hand wrapped itself around my arm, trapping me. "That's it," the man said, yanking on me. "Back to Isolation." It was one of the nurses.

"I don't care," I said, twisting the doorknob one more time for good measure. It wouldn't move.

But at least I'd tried.

Another man grabbed my free arm, pulling me away from the door. I didn't even know how I would have escaped. The elevator didn't come very fast. Were there stairs? And where would I go once I got to the bottom?

It didn't matter. They dragged me back to the Isolation room. I didn't put up as much of a fight, but they didn't seem to care. They still pushed me into the room and locked the door, only to return a few minutes later with some white, fabric contraption. Three of them pinned me down and used the device to tie my arms across my chest at odd angles.

I would learn later that it was called a straight jacket. I guess to "set me straight." All I knew was it hurt and made my arms sorer than the thick brown restraints. They felt heavy from being trapped for so long, like I'd fallen asleep on them.

"Let me go!" I screamed at the top of my lungs. If they were going to torture me and keep me in a cage, I would at least fight back.

The door slammed shut. I was alone. Again, there was no bed in the room. Just an empty, sterile room. There was no bathroom. No window to stare down below at the loading docks. No water or lunch tray.

I kicked the door with my foot, a jolt of pain running up my leg. I missed my shoes. Sock feet were useless.

These people had no problem locking me in their punishment room. They were pros at withholding food or the right to go to the bathroom. I couldn't even wear my own clothes or call my mom.

I was trapped. And I couldn't even use my arms. They had been belted across my chest in a weird spiderweb of white fabric.

Nothing was safe. It was barely my third day, and they had me on some heavy drugs that made me feel like I was a zombie, and I didn't like that feeling at all. And I most certainly wouldn't be allowed to talk to my mom. Not even my dad wanted to talk to me. He'd left me here with no explanation. These mean people with keys and clipboards and rules got to say I was bipolar when I knew the truth. There was no way I was like my mom. And no one would tell me why I was here.

Now I knew I couldn't try to get away. Sure, my attempt had been stupid, and I'd made a fool out of myself. For some wild reason, I had needed to know right then if the door was unlocked.

Slowly, I backed myself up into a corner and lowered myself to the floor. It was tricky; I had to angle myself just right so that my back could touch the wall as I slid myself down carefully. I didn't want to topple over, and I had no way to straighten out my balance since my arms were unusable. When I was safely on the floor, I leaned my head back and tried to make a plan. There had to be a way out of here.

Instead, I fell asleep.

Chapter 14
Not Bipolar

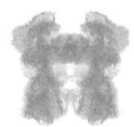

Bipolar.

My mom's face was somewhere in front of me, in the hazy space between sleep and awake. Her sea-blue eyes looked like little pools of ocean, and the pupils were tiny and scared. Her wiry, brown hair framed her face in fractured waves. Those thick glasses with brown rims were too big and made her eyes look even larger than they were. Her face shifted violently as she screamed. "They're trying to hurt me! They want me to take drugs!"

I shook my head. This wasn't real. It wasn't happening again.

It couldn't be real, I told myself, raising my arm in front of my face so that I could study my hand. It was free, untied. No, this wasn't real.

But the memory was. My mom grabbed me by the arm and dragged me from the mobile home where we'd been invited to stay the night. She had left my dad just a few weeks earlier, and we'd been living in our new mountain trailer park. Away from my childhood home, away from my school, away from my dog and cat.

And she hadn't taken just me. She'd taken Nick, too. My mind raced through the trailer park and back to the side of the road, out of sequence. Suddenly, she was standing in front of us again, the moonlight creating shadows on her frightened face. "Stay here." The midnight sky enveloped her as she disappeared into the night.

I wanted to scream, "Don't go!" But I didn't. I stood beside Nick, afraid. I had only been eight, too young to know that something was wrong with my mom. Instead, I looked to Nick for guidance.

But when I turned to face him, his features were expressionless. He wasn't the shocked, scared kid who had sat beside me that night, watching over me while I tried to sleep. Instead, he was the kid who I'd been sitting next to a few days ago, a little older, quieter. Not surprised.

He was watching me in a way that made me wonder... had he known that dad was going to let those men take me? I didn't think so. He was probably just as afraid as me.

We had seen our older brother Kevin get sent away.

David had been kicked out one night, then climbed back into his bedroom overnight using a carefully placed ladder underneath an unlocked bathroom window. He'd been a hero when he'd grabbed his treasured belongings and driven off at sixteen, ready to spend time with friends until his family behaved.

Even my sister Melinda had found her own way out, leaving for a special high school that let her live there, at just fifteen. She was the youngest eleventh grader in her class, and she was gone. It had just been me and Nick. And now it was just him, alone. Stuck in a scary house, not able to tell me what was happening outside of this horrible place.

A metallic sound ripped me out of my dream state. I opened my eyes and blinked rapidly, trying to remember where I was. My arms were glued against me at haphazard angles, my mouth was dry, and my vision was blurred. Above me stood a man in tan scrubs.

Right. I was in the hospital. The Seventh Floor.

"You can't sit in that corner. We can't see you from the window when you sit there."

I squinted my dry eyes as I studied him. I'd stopped crying hours ago, but the heavy lines from tear stains remained on my cheeks. My voice was gravelly from choking back tears. "Or you could let me out."

"Move to the other side of the room."

My back was sore from the position I'd been sleeping in, and I didn't have any way to move my hands. I wasn't sure how I was supposed to get up. "How?" I asked. I squinted to try to read his nametag, but my vision was still blurry.

"You're the one who thinks she knows more than the doc. You'll figure it out," the guy said, stepping back towards the door. "Now move."

I watched as he folded his arms across his chest, tapping the ring of keys against his side with a restless index finger. He was enjoying this. Hatred boiled inside me.

And I needed to figure out how to get from the corner I'd dozed off in and over to the other side of the room. Within sight of the little glass window in the door. In a straight jacket that locked my arms away from me.

Crawling wouldn't work. If I stood up, I might really struggle to get back down, especially with that man looming over me. I wasn't sure what to do, so I shuffled my legs a little in front of me and tried to move my body to the right. Unfortunately, that didn't work. As I toppled over onto my right side, I knew there was no way to catch myself. A gasp escaped my lips, but I was already learning not to scream. Not to cry.

Just to accept life as it came.

I landed with a thud against the linoleum. I felt an echo of the shock against my face as it rolled through my head. All the metal ties on the jacket seemed to clack against the floor in unison, like a tambourine being shaken twice in a school performance. The music died away, and I closed my eyes and sighed. At least the coolness of the floor felt better than the heat of this jacket. Even though my jaw hurt. Even with my arms trapped.

"Move," the man repeated.

I didn't know what the next punishment was. What could be worse than being kidnapped, drugged, or tied up in a coat that held your arms at strange angles? I wasn't sure and I definitely didn't want to find out.

My legs still worked, since they weren't taped against my body or strapped to a bed. I pushed myself up onto my knees, then rolled forward, my stringy hair covering my face. Without hands, I couldn't reach up and push the long strands of hair behind my ears. Instead, they clung to my face, the tears I hadn't realized I was suddenly crying cementing them to my cheeks like glue.

That was how I moved, slowly, like an inchworm. I rolled my body up and pushed forward, smashing my head a few more times along the way before I finally made it to one of the two corners that was visible to whoever needed to check on me from the doorway. By the time I made it to the corner, my tears had worked their way into full sobs, rushing down my cheeks like a tidal wave.

"Stop crying," the man ordered, just as I began to retch all over the floor. I couldn't move out of the way or even wipe my lips. My only option was to tilt my head so that I wasn't lying in my own puke, then roll my body slowly so that I was facing away from the man at the door. It was a weird process that felt more like I was an inchworm, moving my body in odd movements until the untied parts of it could respond just enough to get me away from the smelly mess on the floor.

At least they would be able to see me without entering. Maybe now he would finally leave me alone.

And he did. He left, locking me alone in my isolation room. It was just me, my bad memories, and a pile of vomit. I didn't know how much more of this place I was going to be able to stomach, but I definitely had lost the ability to hold onto my breakfast.

Chapter 15
Caged Air

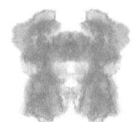

Dreams were a mixture of reality and scary things. That was how the drugs made me feel, like I was weighed down and walking through the space around me. The pills they offered changed, sometimes orange with tiny letters, sometimes pink, and today's pills had been white. Whenever I asked what new meds I was on, I was threatened with Isolation. If I refused to take them, I always got placed back into Isolation. But I'd taken my pills today, and the cloud was weighing down on me. Yet, here I was anyway, in Isolation.

When I awoke the next time, my head was a little clearer. I smiled in spite of my predicament. I felt like the clouds had shifted. My mouth was dry, and when I licked my lips, the residue of regurgitated breakfast made my stomach hurt all over again. But my brain was working right.

I must have thrown up my pills. I decided that I liked the way I felt when I wasn't drugged. I liked being able to tell what was real and what wasn't. I couldn't tell if my vision was back to normal, since I was just staring at the plain, white wall again. I'd gotten used to what it looked like by now, but there was nothing to use to check to see if I was still seeing fuzzy.

"Someday, you'll be free," I told myself. My words sounded like they were coming from a stranger. My throat burned from when I had vomited, and when I ran my tongue across my lips, I could tell they were cracked and broken. I had started chewing on my lower lip when I was nervous, but that was pretty much all the time now. I'd never been like that before the hospital.

I counted to one hundred, then did it again. I repeated one through ten in German, since my sister had taught me the words when she used to live with us. My sister. Melinda. She had been lucky and found a way out of the house ahead of schedule. She had gotten into at a state sponsored high school, the North Carolina School of Science and Mathematics. It was a free boarding school for smart kids. When she left, everything had slowly started to fall apart.

First, my parents had separated. My mom had been parked in front of the house one afternoon when Nick and I got off the school bus. She'd told us to get in, and of course, we had. What other choice did we have?

She took us out to the mountains, where she had rented a small mobile home in the middle of a trailer park. There weren't too many other trailers, and there was a dense forest around us. Our lives had changed all of a sudden.

"I hope Tansy and Sneakers are okay," I whispered out loud. I knew no one could hear me because I was alone, again. I'd gotten so used to spending all my time in isolation. At least when I said their names aloud, they would still feel real. Tansy was our beautiful collie, smaller than Lassie, the dog that was on tv. She had reddish-brown fur and a thin face. Sneakers was our housecat. She didn't like it when we played rough with her. I vowed that I would play with both of them so much once I got home. I would let Sneakers walk all over my back until she was comfortable and sat down. She liked doing that. And I would take Tansy off the horrible chain my dad kept her on and let her run free.

In all the years that we'd had her, I had never understood how terrible she must have felt as she walked around in circles on the long metal chain my dad used to keep her in one place. Suddenly it all fit. My dad wanted to keep everything and everyone in their places. Now that I felt like I'd been chained up and trapped, I got it. I knew the pain that she experienced and I wanted to release her. She should have been free. I should have been free.

I stared at the white paint on the walls. There was a tiny black dot, no bigger than the tip of a pen. If only I had free arms and a paintbrush. The walls needed color. Life. Flowers, animals. A patch of fireflies chasing a kid and her dog.

Closing my eyes, I imagined living in the free world again. I would never take fresh air for granted. Or unlocked doors. Real bowls with real spoons.

Clothes. I wanted to wear a pair of loose shorts and an old t-shirt.

I'd never liked wearing dresses and my legs felt too exposed. I wanted to put on a pair of shorts or pants and hop on my bike. If only I could go soaring down one of the big hills, my feet ready at the brakes, with my hair flying in the wind. Nobody would ever do that in a dress, let alone a doubled-up hospital gown.

There was so much I missed. I just had to figure out what all these grownups needed me to do or say so I could have my freedom back.

Chapter 16
Drugged

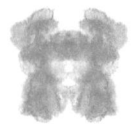

Eventually, I was released again. I spent most of the first two weeks in and out of Isolation. Even after they'd forced me to start taking pills, I was still fighting back. Resisting. Begging for the right to make my own choices. Being DEFIANT.

But that didn't matter. All that mattered was that I was a kid and they were in charge. They were going to break me even if it took forever.

It was almost the end of June by the time I heard another kid taking up my space in the Isolation room. The orderlies seemed to thrive on locking kids in there, and they didn't seem to care which kid it was. Hearing another kid moaning and screaming meant that I was finally free.

I sat in the dayroom, staring at the walls. They were the same merciless white, but at least they had random handprints on them that left the faintest smudges. And there were windows, just on the other side of the room that I wasn't supposed to go near. I stared at the exit door for the millionth time, wishing I had a key. Wouldn't that have been amazing? A way out?

But the drugs made me feel weird, so I didn't do much more than sit in the chair and think. It was hard to carry out a conversation when my mind was short-circuiting.

"I want to go home," I said out loud.

A few teens nodded just enough to let me know they understood. But nobody told me the secret way out. How was I supposed to do or say whatever it was they needed to me to do or say if no one would tell me?

"Are you ready to start working on yourself?" the counselor babbled from across the room. I blinked, realizing we were in the therapy circle.

"Yes," I said. I wasn't lying, I just had no idea what they were asking me to do.

"Very well," he responded, but didn't give me any clues. I lost focus and went back to staring at the walls. At some point, I realized I had a little bit of drool coming out of my mouth.

I wiped away the moisture and glanced up. Group had ended and a few kids were sitting at tables. I was the only one still seated in the therapy circle.

Those meds were too much. I felt heavy all the time, like the world was weighing me down. I needed to stand up and stretch.

When I stood, I realized my hands had started to move a little. Just enough to make me nervous. Were they going to turn me into my mother? I didn't want to take a handful of pills every morning. One pill for the disorder, another for the side effects from the first pill. Another pill, another, another. I'd seen the handful she had to swallow each day, and it was just too much.

I was already nauseous, drooling, and loopy from the pills they'd forced me to take. My vision hadn't improved. And I wasn't sure what they would do to me next. I was at their mercy.

Nobody would let me call my mom. My dad hadn't visited. It was just them and me. And I was powerless.

My legs felt heavy, but I forced myself to start moving. I walked slowly out of the dayroom and into the hallway.

"Where are you going?" one of the orderlies asked.

"Bathroom."

They let me pass, since we were allowed to go to our own rooms for the bathroom during the day. When I finally made it to the room at the end of the hall, I made a choice.

And lay down on my bed instead.

Chapter 17
Silence

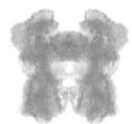

No one ever told me how loud silence was. But I learned anyway.

Night was the worst.

Sometimes I would lie in bed, listening to the distant chatter of nurses and aides at the other end of the hallway. I could make out a few words, but nothing that ever made sense.

Other times, tense periods of quiet were interrupted by screams. They could be shrieks or terror or mania; hard to tell from my bedroom near the end of the adolescent wing. It was the furthest room away from the Isolation room.

I squeezed my eyes shut, trying not to remember my first few days here. Had it really been just a few weeks ago? Back when the only night noise was the rhythmic flow of cars moving up and down Franklin Boulevard?

There were sudden noises, like coughs or the sound of a faraway door opening and closing. The jingling sound of keys as one of the nurses made "rounds" every hour, peeking in the open doorways to make sure no kids had escaped or caused any other mischief.

But there were also regular sounds, the whispering purr of my roommate snoring from across the room or the persistent hum of the air conditioning system. The flickering buzz from one of the hallway fluorescent lights before it would eventually fade to black. Or the beeping of a delivery truck down below, backing into the dock in the hidden part of the hospital. The dreary part I could see from my bedroom window.

Daytime was noise. But so was night.

I stared at the open doorway, the conduit to light from my darkened room. My roommate could sleep through anything, but sleep was becoming a challenge for me.

During the days, I walked around in a groggy state from all the mind-altering meds they forced me to take. Room time in the afternoon often became nap time; I was constantly playing catch up.

I never slept at night, always watching.

Sometimes I thought about the dark circles my mom always had under her eyes. It all made sense now. She'd spent time here, too. My dad had brought her. Just like he'd brought my stepmom.

And me.

I still didn't have answers about why I was here. Answers about how to get out. Just stern glances from adults who assumed I was lying or thought I was a brat. And who knows, maybe I was. I was a problem. A problem child.

I spent the rest of that night replaying past events in my head. If I could figure out what I'd done, maybe I could apologize.

But by morning, all I had was a throbbing headache, tired eyes, and recollections of little things I'd done. Like eating a chocolate bar in the grocery store when I was five or not wearing socks when my dad told me to. Not any of the scary stuff the older kids had done.

Based on what they'd said in group, they were mostly smoking, drinking, doing drugs, having sex, and running away. I'd done none of those things.

And I was still in danger. Being good brought no safety.

Maybe it was time to live up to my dad's greatest fears. Maybe I would become a problem child after all.

Whatever it took to never, ever come back here again.

But that meant I had one huge task in front of me first. I had to get out before I could start worrying about never coming back.

I tried to make myself sleep, even though I spent most of the night staring at my pregnant roommate's belly. I didn't know much about Irene, but I did know that her mom and stepdad had put her in here. That was all she'd revealed in the past few weeks.

Most kids only shared in group. We didn't talk much to each other. What was the point, really? We were here to fix something about ourselves. It wasn't summer camp, and they would never be my friends.

Chapter 18
Dr. Winston

The Adolescent Unit was divided into two sides. The side where all of us lived was separated by a locked set of double doors from the other side, the part where all the doctors and therapists had their private offices. There was a large room that probably got used for family meetings, although I hadn't had any more of those. The last one had been a disaster.

I still didn't know why my dad had left me here.

I was sitting in the dayroom trying to pretend I was zoning out. I'd managed to cheek my meds for the past several days, and I'd only been caught once. Since then, they'd been making me open my mouth way too big and checking me for hidden pills.

That was why I'd had to force myself to throw up my morning pills. I didn't want to be drugged. It was my body; it should be my choice.

The psychologist, a tall man named Dr. Winston, came to get me one morning. He wanted to do some tests on me. All I knew was that they would happen sort of off the unit and that they were supposed to show if I was smart or not. I wanted to show everyone that I was a smart kid, not just another kid with a toxic label of something that wasn't even true.

When I stood up to follow Dr. Winston to his office, my head spun a little. Maybe I hadn't managed to throw up all of the pills. I hadn't been allowed back to the bathroom for thirty minutes after I'd taken them. They kept saying they didn't want us to vomit after taking pills, but they kept giving us pills that none of us seemed to need.

I followed him out of the dayroom and to the double doors. I wasn't sure if there was an easy way to get out from there. A staircase? An open doorway to the outside?

But there wasn't. When we passed through the doors to the other hallway, I learned that there was no exit sign, no flight of stairs waiting nearby. Just a lonely row of doors and brighter carpet than on the adolescent side. The temporary excitement faded; there was no escape. I would just have to take the tests.

Deep down, I hoped that maybe they would prove what I already knew. I knew I wasn't bipolar. I'd seen my mother when she'd abandoned Nick and me by the side of the road. When she destroyed her house, I'd cleaned it up, piece by piece. I'd painstakingly laid out rows upon rows of photographs on towels and newspaper in my dad's basement, hoping they would dry and become salvageable.

Those photos were her memories. Her childhood. She'd lost so much from her illness; I didn't want her to lose the rest of her stories, too. I'd spent hours staring at those photos, wondering about people I'd never met. My parents didn't see their families very much, so we'd been very isolated from cousins, aunts, uncles, and grandparents. I had met my dad's mom, and she'd never liked me. But my mom's mom was a mystery.

I folded my arms over my chest, then immediately released them. No; I still hated the way it felt to hold them against my body, pressed at odd angles that reminded me of the straight jacket. I'd managed to stay out of the Isolation room for a few days, and I didn't want to think about the many ways they had figured out to torture me here.

"You're quiet today," Dr. Winston mused as we stopped in front of a closed doorway. He stuck his key in the lock and opened it, revealing an ordinary-looking office. There was a desk with a nice chair behind it, another chair near the door, and a bookshelf. He had a window behind his desk that overlooked the large parking lot down below. It was the parking lot where regular people parked when they were visiting their families.

I wished my dad would park his car and rush upstairs to rescue me. But he was the one who had left me here to rot. To "get better." Whatever that meant. It was hard to do what everyone expected when I had no idea what they wanted. All I wanted was to be a normal kid, watching cartoons or playing video games. I dreamt of hopping on my bike and chasing Nick and his friends around the neighborhood, trying to fit in with them. Maybe they'd let me go with them to the creek again sometime, where we could search for tadpoles or little frogs. I missed the library and reading books for fun. I hadn't seen a single book in weeks.

I'd heard enough stories from the other kids. They were all older, different from me. They had done things, some of them bad. Most of them had run away from home, smoked cigarettes, or drank alcohol. A few of them were in foster care. My roommate was pregnant, and even though I hadn't had my sex ed class I knew that she must have had sex to get pregnant.

What had I done? I couldn't think of anything worse than stealing a few dimes from my dad's change jar to buy cookies at school. Sure, I'd skipped school a bunch in fifth grade, but I'd stopped when I suddenly had a new stay at home stepmom. My list was short. I hadn't figured it out, and no amount of drugs or therapy circle would answer the question for me. My dad was the only one who could explain what I'd done that was so bad that I needed to be locked away in this terrible place.

I hadn't done anything wild or crazy. Perhaps I liked cartoons too much. I did draw, and I imagined a future as a comic book artist. Most of my drawings were modeled after the Thundercats anyway. I couldn't remember drawing anything that would have gotten me into trouble.

No. I was just a regular kid. Sometimes I argued or didn't want to clean my room, but that was it. I couldn't figure out what I had done that was so awful. I wasn't out of control. I wasn't partying, and I barely had any friends. I just wanted to be left alone. I got good grades in school. I'd even won a few awards; I'd won second place in the school Spelling Bee, beaten only by Nick's best friend. I'd worked hard learning the lists of words, but he'd worked harder. He had even made it to Nationals.

"Have a seat," Dr. Winston told me. I must've zoned out a little. Crap, I didn't manage to throw up fast enough. An orange pill was working its way through my system.

I touched the arm of the chair and lowered myself downward, making sure I didn't fall. The pills made me dizzy, and I was always worried about tipping over. An image flew into my mind, making me squeeze my eyes shut. I didn't want to think about the way I'd felt in the Isolation room that time when I'd thrown up everywhere.

"How are you feeling?" he asked, causing me to open my eyes again.

"The pills make me dizzy. Do I really have to take them?" I asked. Everyone already knew I hated them; I'd made that point quite clear.

His face was a little blurry to me, yet another reason I didn't want to take orange-colored pills for no reason. I stared at him for a moment, willing him to answer. But he didn't. He changed the subject, instead.

"I have some tests for you to do. They're not like regular tests," he began. "They're different. You will look at splashes of ink and tell me what you see."

"Really?" I asked. How could ink decide if I was smart or not?

He opened a folder on his desk, revealing a stack of thick, white cards. The first one had a blob of black color across it. He held it up and asked me to study it.

Chapter 19
Rorschach

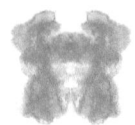

"What does it look like?" Dr. Winston asked as he held up the paper with the weird blob of ink.

I turned my head a little to the side. "I don't know, a lake?" I guessed. It could have been. Maybe it could have represented the lake where we used to swim every summer. Well, every summer except this one. I wondered if my dad got a discount for having one less kid this year. Maybe he'd been getting discounts each year or so, as he'd shed his children. He only had one left at his home by now.

Five minus four was one. Nick was the only one who was still there. I wondered for a moment if he missed me.

I sighed, perhaps a little too loudly. The meds made my thoughts jumble together into wild runaway stories. What would I have given to ditch all the meds and go back to that day when we'd come here for the meeting, but to have woken up with a fever or something that would've prevented me from coming in? What would my life had been like if I'd never been forced to come here for that fake family meeting? Because every way I looked at it, there had only been one goal. The meeting had been to steal me.

He finished scribbling something into his notebook and held up another card. "And this one?"

I giggled. "That's easy," I said, staring at the strange pattern of black that had been splattered across the page. "It looks like a pawprint." Thundercats, Ho! I even got the comic books mailed directly to the house. My sister had bought them for me one year as a Christmas present, and my favorite thing had been to read those comics and then read the fan mail page at the back. I thought about Roxanne again. She'd mailed me a school picture, and I kept it in my little, pink wallet. I'd never even met anyone with a cool name like Roxanne before, and she wrote me letters all the way from the other side of the world! A friend someplace else.

If I could make friends halfway around the world, maybe I could find somewhere else to go. Maybe there was a family that would want me. My dad had dumped me here, and it wasn't like anyone would let me live with my mom.

She was bipolar, after all. The dreaded word these people kept tossing at me like it defined me.

I glanced back up at the psychologist. He was studying my expression, all while writing notes. He didn't even have to look down while he wrote.

"And what about this picture?" he asked, holding up a picture with a large puddle and a puddle that looked like a person next to it.

"I don't know, that could be a person and an animal."

He leaned forward, as if my answer was interesting. "And what is happening with the person and the animal?"

I shrugged, studying the picture. It reminded me of one of those pictures in our encyclopedia set at home. My dad had bought an entire set of those reference books many years ago, and I'd thumbed through the chapters over the years. The books were fun and taught about everything. He kept them next to his National Geographic collection, where I always saw cool pictures about animals that lived everywhere around the planet. "It looks kinda like when a mama cow gives birth, and that person is helping deliver the baby," I said, smiling. I was proud of my answer. He would soon learn just how smart I was.

He jotted down a few quick notes. "And this?" he asked, moving along to another random blob.

I wondered if I would ever draw a scene like this into a comic book. Young girl, imprisoned against her will, trying to outsmart her captors by guessing images in black gobs of paint thrown haphazardly onto paper. "Nothing really. Maybe just a dog." I paused, thinking of my collie at home. Tansy. She had been the runt. I missed her. When I got home, I was going to run around with her for hours. My dad normally kept her chained up in the backyard. Being here had taught me how my dog must have felt, being confined in a little circle of space. "Yeah, it's definitely a dog," I said, looking away. I wanted to give Tansy a big hug and let her lick my face with her slimy, pink tongue. I would even get the comb and clean up her hair really pretty, too. I was going to be a changed kid. Less video games, more outdoors. More playtime with my dog, more time spent riding on my bike, letting the wind blow my hair in all directions as I soared freely.

"This one?"

"A bird."

"And this one?"

I didn't know. I was getting bored, and I wasn't sure I was guessing correctly. The psychologist didn't seem happy with my answers at all. He had started to bunch up his eyebrows the way my dad did right before he started yelling at me.

"A bike. It broke," I said, pointing lazily to a lopsided circle on the page. "That's the broken wheel, right there."

"How did it break?"

How was I supposed to know? "Maybe there was an animal or something in the road and the girl who was riding it had to stop really fast but then crashed the bike into a wall or something." I stretched my arms, suddenly needing to confirm that they were still free. I wasn't in isolation. I wasn't in the cage. My arms weren't weighted down by a straight jacket.

He continued through his stack of cards. My answers blurred together. Farm scenes, kids toys, video game characters. I just saw the things I knew.

"Alright, we have one more test," he told me after he put the cards away. He pulled out a spiral bound notebook and asked me a series of questions. By the time I was done, I felt like all the strength had been zapped out of me. It had to have been an hour straight of back-to-back questions. Some of them made no sense at all, but I just hurried through them. I needed to get back to the adolescent side. I was starting to feel uneasy around this man.

Why was he asking me so many questions?

When he finally closed his materials, I breathed a sigh of relief. Finally.

"Alright, that's enough for today," he said. He stood, so I copied him. "You're smarter than you let on, aren't you?" he asked.

I shrugged. "I get A's in school." I liked being smart. I was in gifted classes at my elementary school. That meant I got to spend time with the gifted group once a week, and we were allowed to play extra video games, like Oregon Trail. I kept trying to make it all the way to Oregon, although I usually died of dysentery in the game. I didn't actually know what dysentery was, though.

We were walking down the hallway, almost back to the unit when he laid it on me. "You're a bit manipulative, I suspect. Your IQ is very high, over 150."

"Is that a good score?" I asked. He was still staring at me. My brain wasn't registering the first thing he had said. Wait. "And what does manipulative mean?"

"Exactly what you're doing now. You're pretending that you don't understand things."

"What?"

He unlocked the door and suddenly grabbed my arm. "She needs more time in Isolation," he said.

"Wait, what?" I demanded. I'd behaved! What in the world had I done wrong?

But it didn't matter. He was the adult. I was the child. He had complete power over me. I would spend the rest of the night trying to decipher the puzzle he'd just dumped in front of me, but all I would see would be white walls.

Chapter 20
Reflections

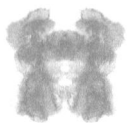

Morning came slowly. It was hard to know for certain that it was morning unless they checked the glass window every hour throughout the night. I had counted fourteen hourly checks.

Isolation was the worst. The room was always too hot or too cold. My back always hurt from sitting against the walls or lying on the floor. They didn't offer pillows or blankets, and they always forgot to feed me.

But they always remembered pill time.

I stared at the little, black dot on the wall again. I'd discovered it a few weeks earlier, the one tiny flaw in their perfectly sterile walls. One of these days, I needed to bring in a paint set and decorate these empty walls. The dot would have been my starting place, and then I could design a world around it.

Of course, painting the Isolation room would only guarantee more time in Isolation. I sighed. There was nothing to do in there except chase my thoughts around in my head.

I played back the whole weird encounter with Dr. Winston in my mind. Was it so awful that I was smart? He seemed angry when he'd finished the tests. Like I'd done something wrong by answering what I'd seen.

Hopefully, somebody would explain to me what I'd done wrong soon, so I could stop doing it. I was tired of Isolation and tired of being in the hospital.

All I wanted was for my dad to forgive me and let me go home. What had I done that was so bad? I rattled off the
different potential offenses. I'd had time to come up with a substantial list by then.

There was my hatred of socks. But I didn't mind them in here, since my feet would get cold if I didn't wear them. They'd stolen my shoes on the day they'd taken me. Maybe I'd just make myself wear them from now on.

I was rude to my stepmom. She had told me point blank that she hated kids after my dad had married her. She'd hated her original set of stepkids, too. She was on her second marriage, just like my dad. Besides, I'd overheard dozens of one-sided conversations between her and her parents or her sister over the phone. I was always the villain in her stories. Why? Because I liked to cook sometimes and I interrupted her when she was in the kitchen. It was "her" kitchen, after all. She'd married my dad, which in her mind made everything hers.

Even though I'd been living in that house long before she'd ever shown up.

I had been mean to my pets. I would be a better pet owner. Tansy would get to run free every afternoon with me, and I wouldn't play rough with Sneakers ever again.

I'd adopted a secret kitten with my friend, and we'd kept it in a shed down the street. That was definitely a bad thing, and it had really upset my dad. I would have to stop doing bad things, even if people were giving out really cute, free kittens with orange hair and adorable, fluffy tails.

Was that why I'd been locked up? Maybe.

Hmm. When I was in first grade, I'd stolen some of my dad's coins from his coin jar and bought cookies at the school cafeteria. Had he counted up all the dimes and realized I'd taken a few of them? Okay, but that wasn't the worst possible thing. Those cookies were amazing, and the chocolate chips melted in my mouth when I ate them. I didn't want to apologize for eating a few cookies. I crossed that one off my list.

I had skipped a lot of school before he'd married Terri. My teacher had been right. I shouldn't have been doing that. But the marriage had cured my desire to have a midweek vacation. There was no way I'd stay home these days. Not unless my stepmom was in the hospital.

I cringed, knowing what that meant. For the first time, I wondered what it was like on the adult side. Was she in Isolation, too? But I doubted adults got punished the way kids were. After all, they didn't have other grown-ups making decisions for them anymore. No, I decided.

She wasn't in Isolation. She was probably just staring at the television and telling everyone what a terrible stepdaughter I was. I imagined her complaining about me in her therapy circle.

My bedroom was never clean. I could try harder to keep it organized. I just hated taking my dirty clothes downstairs until I was ready to wash them myself. My dad had ruined my favorite sweater when he'd washed it with something blue. And my stepmom seemed determined to make all my clothes shrink whenever she told me "they'll drawl up" and forced me to get clothes that were two sizes too big.

I figured I had a sizable list of things to fix. But they just didn't seem that bad. Was my dad really okay with locking me up just because I'd misbehaved? Was I so different from all the other kids? I didn't understand, no matter how many times I'd gone over my list. I was angry,

I'd argued sometimes, I'd been messy, but wasn't that what kids did? Why was I suddenly in need of a "cure?"

Eventually, they would have to let me out of Isolation. Likewise, eventually, they would have to let me out of the hospital. My mom had never been in the hospital for more than a month. That had to be it... I needed to wait for time to pass. Maybe all I had to do was wait.

Chapter 21
Period

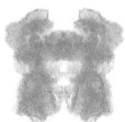

I was sitting in the hallway near the nurse's station in the little chair they always assigned me to after I took my morning pills when it happened. At first, I didn't even notice. My stomach hurt, kind of like the way it used to feel whenever I ate one of my stepmom's meals. Bloody chicken, with red juice seeping from the undercooked meat into the bottom of the tray.

My hand cradled my belly. What had I eaten? They didn't serve anything undercooked in here. It was mostly canned stuff. Or sandwiches. Or little boxes of cereal.

"Can I go to the bathroom?" I asked the nurse who was monitoring me from inside the glass station.

She glanced up and immediately shook her head.

"Please? I don't feel so good," I begged.

When she continued to ignore me, I stood up. I didn't care. I felt like I was going to throw up, but I wasn't quite sure. Something was wrong with my stomach.

"Sit down," she commanded when she saw me launch out of my chair.

I didn't. Instead, I spun on my heel and turned to walk away. I could hear the door opening behind me, and I just knew she was going to toss me back into Isolation. But at that point, nothing else mattered.

I started to walk, the back half of my gown clinging weirdly to my butt. That was strange. I would have run, but as soon as I stood up, I felt like I'd accidentally peed on myself.

What? I was too old to be having accidents.

That made me stop in my tracks. Behind me, the lady approached. "Oh," she said, her voice dropping an octave. "You're on your period."

"My period?" I squeaked. Periods were something I'd read about. They were the kind of thing junior high school and high school kids joked about, and pads would show up on junior high lockers with bright red ink on them. Tampons would thunder out of lockers when they were opened, like pinatas being crushed at a party. "No, I'm not." I didn't have that yet.

"Yes, dear. You are," the nurse said. "Let's get you changed."

I felt dizzy as I walked down the hallway, unsure how she could know something so private about me. Periods were for girls who were living freely, growing up, dreaming of futures. That was pretty much all I knew about them, at least from my weak survey of afterschool specials and articles I'd read in teen magazines. I was still too young for sex ed, after all. And sex ed was the only place to get the period talk, since my big sister was off in college and my mom wasn't really a mom.

She escorted me all the way to my room, then left me there while she went to find a clean hospital gown set for me. I walked into the bathroom, still in a daze. When I looked at myself in the mirror, I didn't feel any different. It was when I turned around to inspect my backside that I noticed the one-inch reddish stain on my gown.

Oh. My. God. What if one of the older kids would have seen me? Mortification rolled through me. This wasn't a celebration. This wasn't a sparkly period pad taped to my locker and my girl classmates teasing me all day long everywhere I went. No. It was a disaster because I had no idea what to do next.

I was still standing there, mouth gaped open, when the nurse returned. She tsked, then said, "It's okay. We'll get you some fresh clothes." She handed me a little, plastic pad. I recognized what it was from commercials, but I'd never held one.

"Um…" I said. "This is my first time."

She tilted her head to the side again, studying me. She looked uncomfortable. "That's okay. You'll have a lot more."

I shook my head. That wasn't what I meant. I just didn't know anything about anything!

"Tell you what. I'll send your roommate to come have a chat with you."

With that, she was gone. I surveyed the damage to my clothes and decided I needed a quick shower.

Chapter 22
Lessons in Girlhood

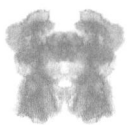

My roommate was waiting for me when I got out of the shower. Irene was seated on her bed, that maternal hand resting on her swollen belly. "So…" she began.

"Yeah," I said, running my hands down the front of my gown to smooth out any wrinkles. At least I was clean. That pad sure felt weird.

"So…" she tried again, letting out a little cough. She looked incredibly nervous. I wondered what words she would use if she was talking to her own daughter, years from now. She had told me she was having a girl. "This is your first period?"

I nodded. I hadn't had "the talk." The whole sex ed talk wouldn't happen until I got back into school that fall. Yet another proof that I was too, too young to be surrounded by older kids on a locked unit. I clutched my arms around my chest, suddenly self-conscious. At least that hadn't changed overnight. What else didn't I know about?

"Well, then, have a seat," she said, pointing to the end of her bed.

"Um, aren't you worried I'm gonna make a mess on that?" I asked, staring at the bright white sheets.

Irene laughed. "No, silly. You've got that pad on."

"Okay," I said, slowly climbing onto the end of her bed and sitting up on my knees. Just in case.

Again, she let out an awkward giggling sound. Something between a chortle and a snort. "Alright. So all girls have periods, as soon as they reach puberty." I needed something to stare at, so I studied the row of cards she had by her bed. Each one had little flowers and tiny writing on it.

I couldn't read the words anymore. My vision used to be good enough to read that far, but that was before the hospital and the pills. Maybe I needed glasses now.

"And the period is kinda like a placeholder, so that if there's a... um... baby that needs to be made, it takes the place of the period."

"You don't have periods?" I gasped. "That's so awesome! I guess it's better to be pregnant."

"Whoa, slow down," she told me. "No. You're eleven. And getting pregnant happens when you have unprotected sex."

"Unprotected?" I wanted to know. Nobody had explained anything at all to me. There were things I kind of knew, but I didn't know very much at all and wanted answers. And it seemed like my roommate was a wealth of information. I wanted her to tell me everything. I didn't even know how to get a boy to look at me like I might be pretty or something.

She shook her head. "Nope. I am not going to have that talk with you today. Today, we're going to just focus on the period part."

I turned my attention back to the blurry flowers. Most of them were pink.

"Periods usually last a few days, and sometimes as long as a week. You have to wear a pad to catch all the blood."

"Am I going to lose a lot of blood?" I asked, thinking back to the ink blots. Was I going to be a big, old blot drawing, lying in a pool of my own blood? I wanted to take the test again. I knew what I would answer for each and every stupid blob of ink. "Am I dying?"

She laughed again, but it was a sad sound this time. "No. It's really not that much."

I glanced at her. Her eyebrows were lifted up like when she got frustrated with me. She was chewing on her lower lip, like I did sometimes when I was nervous. "Okay," I said, because I could tell she didn't want to talk about this any more than the nurse wanted to explain it to me.

"You'll get it every month or so. You just have to stay clean and change the pads every four or five hours," she continued. "And don't even think about that other stuff. You are way too young to have sex."

There were so many questions. I wished I could talk to my sister right then so I could ask, but she was probably too busy studying at her new college. "Okay."

When she was satisfied with her lesson for me, she nodded and stood up, still patting her belly. "Don't have sex. Don't get pregnant," she told me. "When you're too young, other people get to make too many decisions for you."

I nodded, standing up too. She had given me a lot of things to think about. And even though I hadn't understood them all, I did hear that last one, loud and clear.

Chapter 23
Makeup

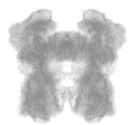

All the girls and two boys sat around the tables, which had been placed side by side for the special guest. Marlee, a local woman who sold makeup, had been invited to the Adolescent Unit to "make everyone pretty."

The same hushed whisper that I'd grown accustomed to filled the room. These kids didn't talk, because none of them wanted to spend the night in the Isolation room.

I watched as the older girls studied the trays of eye shadows and lipsticks. There were sample colors spread out over large pieces of white plastic, with each little box embedded into the large, rectangular design. My roommate picked up a small applicator stick with a fuzzy, white tip that reminded me of a Q-tip. She dipped it into one of the pink lip glosses and dabbed it on her lips.

The only time I had ever worn makeup had been when I was in first or second grade and one of the girls had gotten a makeup kit for Christmas. We had all huddled in the giant cement tube out in the playground, each of us applying large blotches of color to our eyes, cheeks, and lips. When we had proudly shown off our new looks to our teacher, everyone had gotten yelled at. The student with the makeup kit got in the most trouble, though.

I glanced over at Keith. He watched the way my roommate was applying her lip gloss. I wanted him to notice me, too. So, I grabbed my own applicator and reached for a bright red color.

"No, Sheri," Irene scolded. "You should pick a lighter color."

Keith glanced at us for a moment, then looked away. I shrugged and dipped the little wand into a bright pink, instead. I smeared the color across my lips, surprised by how cold it felt. It wasn't that I liked him. I just wanted to not be a dumb eleven-year-old for a moment.

"You're too young for that," she told me.

I stared at her. "Well, I am an adolescent," I hissed. Old enough to be stuck in here. That meant I had to be old enough to wear whatever the older girls were wearing. If she didn't like it, too bad. Besides, I had gotten my period. I'd always heard that meant something. I was supposed to be older or something.

Irene raised an eyebrow at me. I'd been changing, becoming more like the older teens. After all, they were the only people I interacted with anymore. I absorbed info from them like a sponge.

My roommate didn't scold me again. Instead, she ignored me as I let the makeup saleswoman show me how to paint my eyelids and blotch a light pink on my cheeks. When she held up the mirror for me to see my reflection, I gasped.

I looked ridiculous. Like one of those preteens on an afternoon special about trying to grow up too fast. Like when the middle sister on *Full House* tried on makeup to fit in during an unsupervised party. But this was no after school special. Not a party. I was about to wipe the slimy, pink stuff off my lips when Keith looked back at me and smiled.

That was enough for me. I wanted to be adored. I wanted to matter. And after a summer of wasted time and feeling hazy and drugged all the time, what I wanted most was to feel like I was enough for somebody. Enough, not too much. Just right. Like a Goldilocks after school special for kids with bipolar moms and dads who locked their kids away for tiny things, like not cleaning their room or being annoying.

Irene didn't have anything left to say to me when we went back to our room that night. Even though she was older and wiser, I didn't feel like we were meant to be friends. And makeup night had solidified that for me.

Chapter 24
Heavy

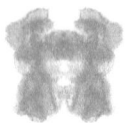

In group the next day, I scanned everyone's faces to see if they were looking at me differently. Nobody was. It didn't seem like they knew my secret, even though it was driving me nuts.

I was in puberty! And it had started at the worst possible place. If I had been home, I would have picked up the phone and called my best friend Erin. At least she would have been able to ask her mom for more details, then share them with me.

"And Sheri, how are you feeling today?" the counselor asked.

I shrugged. "I want to go home," I said, thinking of my best friend. We would hide out in her family's large garage and tell stories about our families. I had so much to tell her after what had happened to me. If only I could get out of this place.

The problem was, I had no idea what I was supposed to do or say to get released.

"That's not a feeling."

I stared down at my sock feet. "Okay. I am sad. I miss my best friend. I want to go home."

"Okay, that's better. Sad. That's a feeling. What do you notice about your body when you feel sad?"

My stomach still hurt, and I was bleeding. How was I supposed to feel?

But when I glanced up at Keith, who was sitting on the other side of the sharing circle, I knew I didn't want to announce how gross I felt to the group. What I really wanted was to feel like somebody gave a crap about me.

Mostly, I just didn't want to feel like a drugged-up zombie, wandering around a locked unit on the Seventh Floor.

"It just feels sad."

"Jackson, help her out," the counselor said. "How does your body feel when you're sad?"

Jackson was a fifteen-year-old boy with spiky, brown hair and a thin mustache. He must have been in puberty, too. He shrugged. "I don't know. Tired." I couldn't remember how long he'd been there. Everything was a jumble.

"I don't feel tired," I said. "I feel heavy, like you're giving me too many pills."

"Sheri," the counselor warned.

I zipped it. There was no point sassing back and forth about pills that some mean doctor was making me take. A doctor who still hadn't spoken to me. He'd come onto the unit and scribbled in my chart a few times, but he'd never bothered to sit down and talk with me directly.

Nobody cared that my vision was blurry or that I wasn't bipolar. Instead, the nurses watching group jotted down everything we said and did in our thick charts, writing notes for the doctors to read about how screwed up each of us were.

They probably could have used some orange pills themselves.

"I have something to say," my roommate said. Everyone turned to stare at her. I couldn't help but stare at her belly. The anti-period. I still had so many questions. "Today is my last day here. I'm being released."

Everyone placed their hands together and lightly clapped.

Well, everyone except for me. Why hadn't she told me she was leaving? Was it because we'd disagreed about makeup the previous night?

And how come I still didn't know how to get out? I'd been there almost a month, and time was flying by with no real answers. I wanted to go home.

Would I have to spend sixth grade up here? Locked away in the highest floor of our hospital, where nobody could find me?

Yeah, I felt sad. Heavy. Like it would take six men to lift me up and drag me away to Isolation if they tried to steal me again.

Chapter 25
Alone

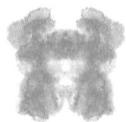

After Irene left, nobody was given her bed. It was just me in a half empty room.

I felt like I could finally stare out the window without someone spying on me. Half the time I really wasn't sure if she was snitching on me or watching out for me.

And now it was just me.

I stared down at the loading docks below my room. There was a delivery truck down there. I couldn't see what they were bringing to the hospital.

It'd been too long since my dad had left me there. I'd given up on my idea of climbing down a rope made of sheets. But that didn't mean I'd forgotten that I wanted to escape.

I knew better than to write or draw anything on paper. Instead, I traced invisible pictures onto the wall beside my bed. Maps. I would figure out a hero's quest, like on Zelda. I would find my own way to survive. Maybe I was never meant to be a part of this family, the one that had abandoned me. Maybe I was supposed to be somewhere else.

Perhaps I'd been given to the wrong family when I'd been born. Maybe the real Sheri was still out there somewhere, living my life. Enjoying two parents who loved her and never getting locked away for an entire summer.

That made me pause. Would I be there for the whole summer? What would happen if they didn't let me out? I hadn't really thought ahead to what I'd say when I did finally get released. Would my classmates know?

"Time for group," a nurse said, hovering in the doorway.

I jumped up, suddenly worried that they'd seen me drawing with my finger on walls. Did that count as bipolar? Would they make me take new meds?

"Okay," I said. I'd learned to keep my mouth shut. It had only taken weeks of Isolation to learn to speak "only when spoken to." But floating around on weird medicines didn't make it too hard to keep my mouth shut.

To her credit, the nurse didn't ask about my finger tracing the walls. At least not directly to me. Who knows what she wrote in my thick chart?

I wandered down the hallway, pausing at the Isolation door. A new kid was in there again, screaming. Maybe they'd be my roommate after they got drugged and released. I hadn't seen them come in, so I didn't know who they were. They might've been a girl. Terrified screams sound the same in the beginning, anyway.

But when I got to group, I found out I'd been wrong.

We were missing one kid at group.

Keith.

The level-headed, smart boy who was always trying to stay out of trouble. The kid who took his pills, answered correctly in group, and never talked back.

What in the world? I didn't understand what that boy could've ever done wrong.

It wasn't until after group that I overheard two of the older kids whispering at the table next to mine.

"Did you hear about Keith?" Miriam asked.

Jackson answered, "Yeah. They finally found a placement for him. It's a group home up in Lexington."

I slumped my chin onto my outstretched arm. Keith was going to leave? And that had made him go to Isolation?

"His mom decided not to pick him up," Miriam said.

"That's so mean. She should've just told him the truth."

I sucked in a deep breath. That was a choice?

My dad could send me away to a group home after I got out of here?

I might never go home again?

That was news to me. And I wasn't sure if I wanted to be sent away or if I wanted forgiveness. Hadn't I wanted to go home? Would my dad take me back? I wasn't even sure. And I might not even find out until the very last minute.

Nothing about this place was fair, though. I was slowly realizing that nobody really cared at all about us kids.

Chapter 26
Trapped

Weeks continued to pass, until I'd already been in the hospital for at least six weeks. Felicia, Irene, Keith, and Angie left, and they had been replaced by other kids. Keith had looked so sad when he'd walked out a few days earlier, his meager belongings bundled into a trash bag.

The newest screamer was Joey, and he sat in group with an angrier face than mine. Everyone who had been there when I'd arrived was gone.

I thought about my roommate for a moment. Irene would have a baby soon. I wondered what would happen to her now that she was out. She hadn't told me anything, not even when we had lain awake in our room at night. She didn't talk about the baby or her parents. She definitely didn't talk about the baby's dad.

Therapy circle was a disaster. I tried to mimic the older kids. Everyone was fourteen or older, and I was the lone eleven-year-old.

"Sheri, what are you working on today?" Dr. Winston asked. He had been scribbling on his clipboard whenever anyone spoke. And suddenly, his eyes were on me.

"I would like to apologize to my dad. I am going to behave better," I said, my words sounding robotic. Memorized. I practiced them in the shower sometimes.

"Very good. What are you going to apologize for?"

I'd already learned that some of my misbehaviors were too silly to apologize for. When I had mentioned the socks, I'd been sent back to Isolation. When I had talked about playing with my pets more, I'd been threatened with another afternoon in the white room. So I had to come up with something bigger. Something badder.

"I will not be mean to my stepmom. I should be obedient to her."

"Good, good. How does that make you feel?"

Terrible. Like a liar. I hated her. "Sad. I should not have been mean to her. She was kind enough to marry a single father. She deserves a chance."

She didn't. I knew that. She had to know that. But bringing up my truths was pointless. I'd been in Isolation far too often. I'd kicked and screamed and cried and vomited and peed in that room. I didn't want to go back in. I wanted to go home.

I wanted to be a normal sixth grader. Although, how would I ever be "normal" again? Now that I knew this place existed, my life was forever changed. I would always be in danger.

"Well?"

"Huh?" Oops. I'd gone off on one of my thought spells again. The meds didn't let me maintain my focus, but that would just get me in trouble. It was a constant loop of danger.

"What changes are you willing to make?"

"All of them."

"Such as…?"

I stared down at my hands. The plastic bracelet around my wrist looked a bit grimy. Was it really July? Had I really been here over a month already?

I shrugged. I didn't want to go to Isolation. I'd been able to stay out of that room for almost a week. All I had to do was stay semi-drugged and answer a few questions in group. Otherwise, I stayed quiet.

That's what this place was training us to be. Quiet, frightened kids. Kids who would never speak up for themselves. Because whenever we did, we were punished.

Fine. I would be that kid.

"I'll be nice to my stepmom. I'll clean my room. I'll wear socks."

Dr. Winston raised an eyebrow at my last one, but it was a huge issue between me and my dad. So what if I didn't have a laundry list of bad things I would avoid? I wasn't fourteen. I was eleven! Sometimes I wanted to scream my age at him so he would remember. These kids were mostly in high school, and I was barely about to start my last year of elementary school.

"Okay."

He wrote something down, then moved on. I looked away. There was no point squinting to figure out what he wrote in his notes about me.

Instead, I zoned out.

Chapter 27
Summer Concert

"We have a special treat for all of you," Nurse Brandy said the next afternoon. I turned towards the woman's voice, halfway curious. A special treat could mean something awful or something surprisingly normal.

And I never knew which one to expect.

I'd seen other adolescents come and go. But I stayed there, still waiting for whatever "treatment" I was supposed to be getting to make me acceptable enough to go home.

"We're going to watch a concert on the lawn."

"A concert?" someone asked.

What? A concert? On the lawn? Like, outside?

My thoughts raced from *Oh, I wish I'd skipped my pills so I could run away* to *Wow, I'll get to breathe air and touch blades of grass* to *I hope the music isn't horrible.*

"Yes," the nurse continued. "It's our July 4th celebration."

"Wasn't July 4th a couple of weeks ago?" someone groaned.

"It was," Brandy told us. "But we decided to celebrate anyway. Better late than never."

Fireworks? A concert? The only thing that would top a few hours of outside time would be permission to go home. But at that point, I'd take anything I could get. A stolen summer was a long time for an eleven-year-old to stay cooped up on a psych ward, waiting for someone to realize they'd made a mistake.

We were given dinner and told that we had to be on our best behavior. I wondered if Irene's baby had been born yet. I thought about the group home Keith had been sent away to. Maybe he would meet my brother. Or not. I tried to calculate how old Kevin must have been by then, either seventeen or eighteen.

That got me thinking. Where did kids go after foster care? And if they got sent away, did that mean that there was suddenly an available bed? Like in my room, now that Irene had left? I did know that it had taken Keith a week to get placed in the group home, because they'd been waiting on a bed.

I wasn't sure if having a bed available meant that a kid got sent home or ran away. If the group home was anything like the Seventh Floor, I imagined beds became available more often when kids ran away, because our parents weren't coming back for us.

When it was time for the concert, a handful of extra nurses and orderlies showed up to help watch us. I walked in the single-file line that they made us form, eyes straight ahead, wondering if there was any way to escape.

But the repetitive question I'd struggled with when I'd arrived rolled through my mind again. I wasn't a cute five-year-old anymore. Where would I go? Would there even be any parents out there who would consider taking in a kid like me? After all, I was drugged. I was broken. I'd been labeled crazy. "Bipolar."

No, I decided. I didn't have many options. But that didn't mean I wouldn't run.

It just meant that if I did, I really didn't have a plan.

We walked out the double doors that had kept me trapped inside this horrible place since the day of my family meeting. The hallway was one long corridor that connected to the adults' side. To my right, a smaller hallway reached the door from our dayroom. The door that was always locked.

We continued walking to the middle of the hallway, where there were several elevators. One of the nurses pushed the button to summon the elevator. How many nights had I dreamt about getting into this elevator?

The door opened in front of us. Everyone piled in, squishing me in the back corner.

I watched as we soared downward, the number rolling backwards from seven all the way to one. It didn't stop on any of the other floors.

We were full, anyway. We wouldn't have had room for extra passengers.

The staff lined us up again and had us walk in our single-file line. Away from the front entrance, towards some unknown part of the hospital. We ended up in a corridor that looked plain, like it was just for staff. At the end of it, there was a door.

When we reached the door, one of the staff members unlocked it with a key.

Each of us stepped out into the great outdoors. We were on the loading dock, but it smelled like we were in the mountains. The air felt suddenly lighter. Crisper. Like it was free.

I wanted to be free.

"Remember what we said," Brandy reminded us. "No wandering off. Everyone stays together on the blankets."

Blankets? I wasn't sure what she was talking about until we started walking around the next corner. There was a small hill covered in fresh grass, but there were four evenly spaced blankets spread out on the lawn.

The other kids sat down, so I sat down too. At least I was outside. I felt like the air would melt right through me. I'd never cherished it like this. I'd spent my childhood running around outdoors, but I'd never understood that the freedom of fresh air was fuel for my soul.

Instead, I'd felt a summer inside an industrial psych ward. Everything had been fake, from the fluorescent lights to the pretend smiles of staff members. The air had been spat out by air conditioners, recycled into the room over and over. It probably carried our tears in evaporated form.

I'd been frozen inside, even in the heat of summer. Chilled. That's what this place did to us. It turned us into ice and then hung us out for the staff to watch us melt.

Chapter 28
Elvis Impersonators

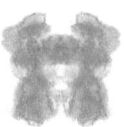

We sat outside on the blankets for at least twenty minutes before the singers showed up. They had brought in three men dressed as Elvis. Each one of them had sparkly adornments all over their outfits, and their hair was slicked back in unison.

I had never liked Elvis because my dad liked him. My dad enjoyed 50s music. It had stopped being enjoyable after my dad had started being mean to me. That... had been around six months ago, when he'd gotten married.

But that night was a special treat. I kept gulping in all the air my greedy lungs could inhale. Smelling the freshly cut grass. Running my hands through the tiny blades at the edge of the blanket.

Several adults had joined us from the other side of the Seventh Floor. My stepmom wasn't one of them, but that didn't surprise me. Knowing my dad, she was probably home already. I was the one that would stay behind.

I considered my options. It was getting darker, and we were behind the hospital. I could hear the distant sound of the closest street. Cars drove by, unaware of the imprisoned kids who had been let out for air and awkward Elvis songs.

"Like a river flows, surely to the sea," the Elvis in purple sequins crooned into his microphone.

The Elvis with a golden jacket chimed in, "Darling so it goes," and I whispered the chorus along with all three of them, "Some things... are meant to be."

I knew the words. Of course, I did. I'd grown up
hearing each and every one of them.

Some things... were meant to be. I glanced back behind me.

There was a hill leading towards the road. And there were a dozen staff members. They looked strong, athletic.

I'd never make it. One of the staff from the adult side locked eyes with me. I immediately turned back to the front. Nope. I would not be able to escape.

Instead, I laid face down on the blanket and let myself breathe in all the scents. I picked a tiny clover. It only had three leaves, so no wishes. I spread out my fingers, searching for one with four leaves.

No such luck.

The heaviness from my meds took over, and the songs lulled me into a state of sleepiness. It wasn't peaceful, but it felt nice to relax in the cool summer breeze.

Around me, everyone else was in their own little world, too. There were no fireworks because July 4th had come and gone. We were a few days away from August. Summer had drifted by, and I'd spent most of it inside an Isolation room or pretending to care in therapy circle.

I hadn't seen my dad all summer, and they hadn't let me talk to my mom. All I knew anymore was this life. Threats of punishment. Forced meds. Weird side effects. Tummy aches. Teens who had told me how and why they'd run away.

Teens who had taught me how to forget the things that hurt. They'd droned on and on about their bad choices. They'd told the same stories in group, asked for the same apologies. But one thing had been made clear.

Eventually, the older we got, we would each have more and more that we needed to forget. And these kids had given me some bad ideas about things I could do to pretend away the bad memories I was creating in the hospital.

Sure, I'd arrived as an innocent eleven-year-old who had only wanted to play video games and had scoffed at the "bad" things that older kids did. But if I was going to face the same punishments, why not just do the bad things, too?

The three Elvises kept singing, and I kept running through the laundry list of bad ideas I'd collected. After all, I'd been lost in my thoughts all summer. That night wasn't any different. It was just outside.

Chapter 29
Man in the Mirror

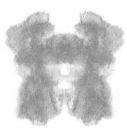

A gray boombox beckoned to us. The soft beat of a musical song I didn't recognize came on, capturing my attention. I glanced up, trying not to move too quickly. Slow movements. Nothing too sudden, or else they might think I was going to do something crazy again.

I walked past the doorway to the Isolation room. It was currently unoccupied. Available. I'd stayed out of it for several weeks. The last thing I wanted to do was find my way back inside.

Michael Jackson's voice beckoned to us. I slipped into the small "family room" and sat on one of the sofas. A short kid with bright red hair and pimples sat beside me. I didn't remember his name. At some point, I'd stopped trying to figure out who everyone was.

We were dramatically quiet. Like prisoners. Only new kids needed to be told the rules: never speak, never argue, never stand up for yourself, never move too fast, never refuse your meds, always say a feeling word, always apologize even if it wasn't your fault.

I stared at the boombox. My vision split it into two identical boomboxes. I squeezed my eyes shut for a moment, trying to get my eyes to work right again. My absentee doctor had changed around my meds again, and I'd been feeling the difference.

As I reopened my eyes, I saw one boombox. Beside it was one of the nurses. She pressed play while Dr. Winston sat in the background, taking notes again.

"This is called Man in the Mirror," she said, as if that was supposed to mean something to any of us. But a few kids were bopping their heads up and down, like they recognized the song. I didn't know it.

I leaned my head forward, looking down. I immediately was on edge as Michael began to sing. By the time he hit the chorus, my hands were trembling.

"I'm starting with the man in the mirror. I'm asking him to change his way," Michael sang. I clasped my hands together to keep them from shaking too much. They felt sweaty and seemed to move on their own.

It had to be the lithium. I would stop that one as soon as I got out of the hospital. If I got out.

As the song continued, I tried to concentrate. It was so hard. The song felt like a dagger being stabbed at each of us. What they were saying was loud and clear.

We were at fault. We were here because we were bad kids. We had to look in the mirror and figure out what we needed to change about ourselves so that we would be "good enough."

I glanced up in time to see Dr. Winston watching me. He was writing while he stared in that creepy method he used. He never had to look down while he wrote.

The song finished, and the nurse pressed rewind. I waited as she prepared the song for another round.

"Today, I want each of you to write down on a piece of paper what you're going to change. Listen to the song again and make a list."

Crap. I needed a list. Everything was hazy. I couldn't write my real list.

But I knew it by heart. I would figure out how to escape. I would leave that horrible house. Maybe I'd end up in a group home like Keith. Maybe I'd convince my brother to take me in. Maybe I'd just be a lowly runaway. I didn't care. I knew I couldn't ever trust my dad again.

The staff members passed around blank sheets of paper and pencils. They would collect those pencils later so that nobody could hurt themselves. But for now, I had a piece of paper and a writing instrument.

And I didn't write down my real list. Instead, I slowly wrote out the words that I'd convinced myself I had to say.

"I will behave. I will listen to my dad and my stepmom. I will do my chores. I will get good grades. I won't talk back. I will clean my room." I stared at my list. It was all actions, no feelings. I knew I'd never get away with a list like that. I tapped the pencil on my paper, noticing how Dr. Winston was watching me again. I carefully wrote a few more sentences: "I will talk about my feelings. I will pay attention to how I behave when I am sad and angry. I will go to therapy and take my meds."

Lies. Whatever.

I handed in my assignment and pencil. Maybe it would be enough. I'd learned what to say. They'd taught me to pretend I was okay even though I was the complete opposite of fine.

The song played nonstop for the whole therapy session. I was so grateful when it was time to go to bed that night. I never wanted to hear that song again.

Chapter 30
August

Only a few days had passed before they gathered all of us back into the family visitation room. The staff were antsy, pacing around like they were worried about something.

The nurse flicked on the television, and across the screen it said, "Breaking News." There was video footage of a map showing the Middle East. A tiny country, Kuwait, had been invaded by their larger neighbor, Iraq. News images were grainy and showed plumes of smoke rising into the sky. Some of the older kids sat at the edge of their seats.

"What does this mean for us?" I whispered to Joey.

"They'll probably call a draft."

A draft? Like back in Vietnam? "Does that mean they'll make my big brothers go?" I hissed back in his direction.

He shrugged. "Maybe." I watched as he squeezed his eyes shut. "I'm almost eighteen. They might call me, too," he said.

Joey leaned back in the sofa chair, trying to distance himself from me and the conversation. I'd seen him zone out a lot of times. It was something he'd learned right away, even though it had taken me handfuls of meds and at least a dozen times in Isolation to figure out.

I watched the same footage, over and over. The newscasters didn't have much, so they played it on repeat. They taught us where Kuwait and Iraq were located.

As I stared at the television, anger boiled inside me. While these horrible adults had been drugging us and blaming us for whatever had happened in our houses, the world outside had moved on. People's lives had continued on the outside. Wars had started. People had been born and died.

My summer had been a waste. I'd learned to cheek meds, how to run away, and that older kids used alcohol to numb their pain. Well, older "bad" kids. But everywhere I looked, the kids seemed fine. It was the adults that seemed to have anger issues.

Especially Dr. Winston. He was the one who had punished me for being too smart. I'd learned what he'd meant by his mean "manipulative" comment. He'd thought I was faking it when I didn't know things.

I hadn't been. But one thing was for certain, I'd learned plenty over this horrific summer.

"Two of my brothers are old enough to be drafted," I said softly. Joey came out of his haze and stared back at me.

"I'm sorry."

"I don't even know one of them," I whispered. "My dad sent him to foster care a long time ago. I don't even know where he is."

There wasn't much he could say to that. We'd all become the awkward sibling that could get sent away. I was now in the same precarious situation my brother had been in.

But something had changed. The air had shifted. There was something about a looming war that made everything feel different.

And I was right.

Chapter 31
Released

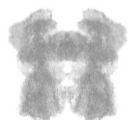

"You're going home today," the doctor said the very next day. I stared down at my hands, not sure how I was supposed to react.

Nothing felt different. It didn't feel like anything had changed. I was still the "Problem Child" who didn't like wearing socks or cleaning my room. I still hated my stepmom. My dad had barely visited me, and I was angry that he'd left me here for so long.

But there was no way I would dare say that to Dr. Reddy. The first and only time he'd bothered to actually speak to me was on my release day. He was letting me leave, and I was going back home. That was that. I didn't want to stay. But I didn't want to go back with my dad, either.

When my parents had first separated, I had convinced myself that the judge would let me live with my mom. After all, the only kids I knew with divorced parents always lived with their moms. I hadn't expected for him to get custody. He didn't seem like he was too interested in being my dad, anyway. I'd heard him tell me more than enough times that he'd only wanted four kids. Those words had played on repeat in my head when I'd been in Isolation.

I sighed, not sure what to expect. Would he keep forcing me to take the pills that made my head spin and my vision blurry? Would everyone know where I'd spent my summer? I didn't want anyone to know. Deep down, I was terrified that the kids at school would figure it out and stop talking to me. I was already a weird kid who didn't really fit in. I only had one close friend at school, my neighbor Erin. I wasn't sure what she would think of my summer in the hospital. After all, I'd been isolated for the whole summer. The only kids I'd seen were also stuck up here.

My dad came to pick me up a few hours later. He didn't seem too excited to bring me home, but I knew better than to ask him anything. What if he changed his mind? What if he made me stay?

I walked back down the long hallway one last time, heading back to my already clean room. I'd left all my belongings in a brown paper bag on my bed. There was no reason to keep any of my sketches or poems. They sat at the bottom of the trash can, ripped into tiny shreds. All that I needed were the few personal items I'd been allowed to have and the clothes I was holding in my hand. They hadn't even trusted me to get dressed in real clothes until my dad had arrived.

And then they handed me back my outfit from that day back in June. Washed in industrial soap and left somewhere to rot for the rest of summer. I sniffed the faded yellow shirt before putting it on. It had been my favorite when I was younger, a hand-me-down from my big sister. There were several blue and silver heart outlines on it, each with peeling paint. The material stretched too thin, and now that I was an Adolescent, I was all-too aware of the changes that had been happening with my body. It didn't fit the way it used to over my chest, and I didn't like it. I suddenly wondered if I would need a training bra before school was back in session.

My shorts felt shorter. I'd been stuck in the weird double-hospital gown all summer, so I hadn't picked up on changes in legs. But I'd grown a little taller, too. I walked over to the bathroom mirror, the same spot where I'd stared at myself for too long with bright pink lipstick. Sure, I was eleven, but a part of me wondered if I was more alike or different from the kids who had raised me over the summer.

I wasn't the same person who'd been dragged in here, kicking and screaming. I was someone completely different. Someone who knew more truths than before. I understood what kind of place Kevin had been sent off to. I knew those places might capture me, too. And there was nothing I could do to stop the impending sense of doom that was rising in my chest.

A sturdy knock at the door reminded me that my dad was waiting. I was sure he'd be annoyed that it had taken me so long to change, but would that mean he'd change his mind? I quickly gathered up the two faded gowns and cracked open the door.

The nurse standing at the other side put her hands on her hips and smiled. "You'd think you were trying to stay," she said, winking conspiratorially.

I shook my head quickly. "No. Just trying to get used to wearing real clothes again." She took the gowns from my hand and studied me. I automatically tugged the shorts downward a little bit, but they still felt too tiny.

"I remember the first time I saw you," she said as we walked slowly up the hall. "You were about this tall," she said, indicating below her waist, "and you were so scared. You were visiting your mom on the other side."

I tilted my head to study her. No, I wasn't. I didn't remember ever visiting my mom up here. But I didn't want to contradict the lady who had keys. I needed to leave.

I needed to smell fresh air.

And I would do whatever it took to never get locked up again.

As we passed the closed door for the Isolation room, my heart thudded rapidly in my chest. Never, ever, ever. I didn't want to think about the countless hours of growing up I'd done in there. I just wanted to leave and pretend this whole thing never happened.

Or leave and find my own way. At that moment, I glanced up and saw my dad. He was standing at the end of the hallway, his arms folded over his chest. He had that impatient look on his face, the one that told me exactly how he felt. He'd been up here picking up his wives and now his youngest kid far too many times.

"Ready to go?" my dad asked.

I shrugged. It wasn't like I wanted to spend the rest of my childhood here. "Yes," I said, even though I didn't have any idea what to expect anymore.

The nurses unlocked the main set of double doors. I stepped off the unit for the first time since the Elvis concert, not quite sure what to expect. Would the orderlies swoop in and grab me again if my dad changed his mind?

But it was still just an ordinary hallway, with a tired, old carpet connecting the distance between the Adolescent Unit and the Adult Unit. In the middle, the elevators were right where I'd left them. My dad approached them nonchalantly, already ignoring me again. There was no hug, no "I missed you." No celebration of my newfound freedom. Instead, it was more of the same.

Except before he'd left me here, I'd been blissfully unaware. I'd been okay with his long periods of silence and random spouts of anger, because at least I'd never been truly his target. As he pressed the elevator button and gave me a strange look, I knew that had changed. I wasn't hidden anymore.

I had always wanted for him to see me. To want to spend time with me. To take me on bike rides or to toss a ball around at the park. But this, well, it was different. I wasn't a prized child. Instead, I felt dirty. I'd been labeled.

The doctor had sworn I was "bipolar" like my mom. That was the only thing that made sense to him, and he'd felt confident throwing pills at me like that would change me. The psychologist thought I was "manipulative." But that wasn't true, either. After two months and ten days, I would have expected something to have finally fit. A label, a diagnosis, a name for something. But nothing did. Because maybe nothing was actually wrong with me.

In front of us, the elevator doors opened. I swallowed hard, still terrified that he might change his mind. Worried that a group of men in scrubs would come grab me and tie me down.

At least I had learned to not fight them. There was no point; they were stronger than me anyway. I had learned to just take whatever life threw at me. If it was Isolation, or meds, or whatever else, I'd lost that fight. I hadn't spoken to my mom in months.

I glanced up at my dad, wanting to ask if I could see her. Knowing that I couldn't ask, at least, not here. Instead, I followed him onto the elevator, tucking the brown bag under my armpit. I definitely didn't like holding my arms over my chest anymore. I'd been in that straight jacket more times than I could count.

The elevator managed to stop at every single floor. A few hospital employees glanced at the little plastic wristband that I was still wearing. I hadn't been allowed to remove it upstairs, so I figured I would wait until I was home.

I leaned back against the elevator wall, letting other passengers crowd into the space where I had just been standing. There were a dozen people in there by the time we reached the first floor. I was just out of reach of my dad, and honestly, I wasn't sure I wanted to stand too close to him anyway.

But the people scattered, and it was just me and him again. We walked towards the exit. Past the information desk, past the row of empty chairs. We didn't stop at the gift shop. There weren't flowers or balloons that could fix broken kids.

I bit my lip. Was I broken? I wasn't sure.

We reached the set of electronic double doors. They whooshed open, exposing an outside world that I'd only seen once in my time here. During the fake Elvis concert.

The sun was shining bright in the sky, brighter than I would have expected for mid-August. "When does school start?" I dared to ask as we walked towards the parking lot. I knew better than to ask about school shopping or new clothes. New school years always meant sifting through my older sister's clothes from back when she was my age. My dad kept labeled boxes in the basement over the years.

"Monday," he told me.

Monday.

Chapter 32
Home

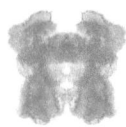

Home wasn't like I'd remembered it. When I got back, it didn't feel like my home anymore.

Terri was in the kitchen, probably undercooking something. It was too early for lunch, and I wasn't hungry anyway. Just smelling her cooking reminded me that I hadn't had those stomachaches from food. Just from medicine.

I walked through the kitchen and into the dining room, where the large table looked the same. My dad kept his newspaper and reading glasses at one end. To the left was the door to the sunroom, a tiny room that had been added to the house many years ago. Our house was one of the oldest ones in our small town, and the first one that had electricity. But when I glanced in the direction of the sunroom, the door was closed. There was a new lock on the door, near the top.

He'd put a lock? Why?

I turned the other way, instead, walking through the living room. Nick was camped out in front of the television, watching a cartoon I used to like. "Hi," I said.

Nick didn't look up. Instead, he kept his eyes locked on the screen. "Hi."

The empty feeling in the pit of my stomach grew. I clutched the brown bag under my arm even tighter, then moved towards the stairs. Away from my dad who left me there in the hospital for so very long, away from the new lock on his door, away from the stepmom who hated kids, away from my brother who didn't even seem to miss me. I wanted to take the stairs two at a time and get as far away from everyone as I could, as fast as possible. But I also knew they were all probably watching me to make sure I was less crazy. Or whatever.

I touched my free hand to the banister and walked up the stairs slowly. One step at a time. No running. No sudden movements.

When I reached upstairs, I saw my cat sitting on the hallway floor. Sneakers. She had the same white fur with black splotches that I remembered. Her forehead had an upside-down V shape on it, with dark hair over her head in an almost human pattern. She was old by then, and Nick and I had goofed around too much with her when she was little. She glanced up at me, her light green eyes studying me without recognition. Her little pink nose tilted up, sniffing the air, but she didn't seem too excited.

"You, too?" I asked softly but moved on. I pushed open the door to my small room and stepped inside.

There were three bedrooms upstairs; the first one was across from the bathroom, and it was tiny. The middle one was larger and had been used whenever two kids had to share a room. The last one was small and had been David's for so many years that I could barely think of it as Nick's room. I'd shared the middle one with Nick, then with Melinda. Over the years, I'd moved back and forth between the middle and the small room across from the bathroom.

But when I opened the door to my old bedroom, the room had changed. The bed was covered in my dad's boxes. S-gauge trains. He'd been a collector since he was a kid, and his trains were off-limits.

I hovered in the doorway for a moment, taking it in. Not only had they sent me away, but I'd been moved. I sucked in a deep breath, trying not to let myself feel strong emotions. Maybe that was why they'd sent me away; maybe I just needed to learn not to feel sad when it felt like I'd just been sucker-punched in the gut.

After I shut the door, I spun around, causing Sneakers to stand up and walk away. She gave me a strange look before heading downstairs.

There was no way he'd given me David's old room, so I walked over to the middle room. Sure enough, all my things had been dumped unceremoniously in there. There were two beds in the room, both unoccupied. My old toys had been tossed in a box and left in the middle of the room. I walked to the closets. The first one was filled with boxes. They weren't mine. I moved to the second closet, where I found my clothes. Some had been hung up, but most were in a hamper at the bottom of the closet. I reached into the row of hanging shirts and pulled out a larger shirt. In the hamper, I found my old basketball shorts. At least they weren't so tiny and tight.

I quickly changed out of my too small clothes, then tossed them in the back of my closet. I didn't want to think about where I'd been or any of the other places the older kids had told me about. What I wanted most was to pretend that nothing had changed. Nothing.

I laid down on the bed and stared up at the ceiling. I could do nothing at all. Or, maybe, I could call Erin. But what would I say? I wanted to talk to my mom, but I also didn't. That nurse had remembered me? I didn't remember visiting that place at all when my mom was there. All I remembered was going to the airport once to pick my mom up, after she'd been up in New York visiting her aunt. For so many years, I'd believed she was away, visiting family. I'd only known about her illness since I was eight.

And that had changed me.

Now, I knew even more. I understood why she didn't trust anyone. I most certainly didn't. And somehow, I was going to have to get it together and go back to school, like I hadn't just spent the whole summer locked up in a strange place. Like I hadn't learned about periods and boys from kids who were supposed to be crazy. From where I had been sitting, they'd seemed mostly okay to me.

Chapter 33
Sixth Grade

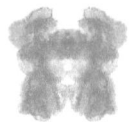

School started a few days later. By then, I'd learned that everything had changed. If I spoke up, I was threatened with returning to the hospital. If I raised my voice, "I'll send you back," my dad would say. If I didn't finish my dinner, same thing.

My dad had handed me a few orange pills that morning, but he didn't know that I knew how to cheek them. I spit them into my hand when he turned away, then shoved them into my pocket. I was done being medicated. And I wouldn't be going back to the Seventh Floor.

I walked into Sherwood Elementary School with new resolve. When I was five, I'd failed at running away. But now, I was eleven, wiser, and I had a plan. Someday, I would leave. And that someday would be soon. Very soon.

When I stepped onto campus, I realized that nobody knew what had happened to me over the summer. Nick was in junior high now, and sixth grade was the oldest grade at my school. It was before all the elementary schools got converted to middle schools, before the high schools absorbed the ninth graders into their programs.

All I had to do was stay out of trouble and figure out how to get out of this place. That would be a lot easier without a pesky big brother reporting everything I did or said back to my dad. Nick had changed while I'd been gone.

My brother was watching me constantly, like he expected me to do something crazy. Like break all the windows and spray mustard and ketchup on the walls or leave all the lights on with money and food on the table. But I wasn't crazy, and I definitely wasn't ready to get sent away again.

My assigned seat was in the back row of Ms. Stowe's sixth grade class. I had been looking forward to being a sixth grader for so long, but now everything felt flat. The words on the board were hard to see, but I could squint my eyes just right and figure them out if I tried hard enough.

Everyone around me talked about the wonderful things they'd done all summer. I didn't want to talk about what I'd done. I wasn't even sure if I was allowed to, since my dad had told me not to.

When each of us was called on to talk to the class about our summer vacation, I didn't speak. I just let the moment pass. I could pretend to be shy. That was safer than telling everyone my dad had sent me away.

Besides, who would have believed me? If I hadn't experienced it myself, I wouldn't have believed it either.

Chapter 34
Dirty Blonde

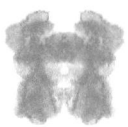

School lunches were familiar. There were octagon-shaped pizzas with unnaturally bright orange cheese, mystery meat patties that looked like they were supposed to be hamburgers but tasted like old shoes, and macaroni noodles mixed with weird sauce and tiny meat crumbs.

By the end of the first week, I was considering switching to peanut butter and jelly sandwiches for the rest of the year. Except my dad would notice if I started making sandwiches. He kept tabs on the groceries and chewed us out if we ate something too quickly or if we used something that cost too much. Home sweet home.

I'd been trying to figure out how to save money for my escape, and I'd come up with a genius plan. If I brought a bagged lunch, they wouldn't make me spend the dollar and ten cents my dad gave me for lunch on a gross hot meal. And if he didn't know I was packing sandwiches, I could save all that money for whenever I finally built up the courage to leave.

When I was standing in the lunch line the following week, ready to buy my weekly cookie instead of a meal, Malorie ended up two kids ahead of me. She was standing next to some of the cool kids, and she had a smirk on her face. "Hey, Sheri," she said, causing me to glance over at her. She had fresh braces, and her red hair was pinned into a perfect French braid. "You're a dirty blonde. Did you know that?"

The kids around her giggled. I shoved my hands into my pockets, trying not to think about my hair or that she had just called me dirty in front of everyone. What did she know? Had someone told her about the hospital?

I didn't know what dirty blonde meant. But I left the line and didn't buy a cookie. I sat down at the table and didn't open my brown lunch bag, either. Even when the teacher's aides walked around to check on us, I just sat there.

There was nobody to talk to. I didn't have anyone I could ask about the mean words Malorie had said. That girl had never been nice to me, anyway.

The dirty blonde hair swam in front of my face. I pushed a long strand of hair behind my ear, trying not to think about it. But it was all I could think about. "Dirty blonde." The words were running on repeat in my head.

I'd managed to save twelve dollars so far, since I'd mostly been eating mushy peanut butter and jelly sandwiches. When I was walking home later that day, I stopped in the drug store near my house. I moved quietly through the aisles, trying not to rush too quickly to the hair dye aisle.

Suddenly, I found myself surrounded by hundreds of boxes of hair dye. Each one had a smiling, happy woman on the cover. The hairstyles were flawless, and each color was bolder than the one next to them. I ran my hand through my hair, considering my options. If I dyed my hair something too dark or too different, my dad might send me away again.

Maybe I would just make my hair less dirty. Less institutionalized. My hair must have lost some of its color from being cooped up inside all summer.

I finally chose a seven-dollar box of platinum blonde
hair color. The girl on the cover had shiny teeth and bright blue eyes. Her smile was infectious, like a self-made woman who didn't have a care in the world.

When I walked over to the register, nervousness worked its way through my body. My fingers were fidgety, and my heart was racing.

Would the cashier let me buy this?

I decided I needed a distraction. Quickly, I grabbed a pack of candy and placed it on top of the hair dye when I set my items on the counter.

The cashier was an older lady who did not have dirty blonde hair. Hers was mousy brown, almost like the color my stepmom kept dying her hair. I definitely didn't want brown hair, because I didn't want to look anything like Terri.

"This is for you?" the lady asked.

I nodded, fear rising in my chest. My stomach did a little flip flop.

"Aren't you a little young for this?"

I took a deep breath, then spilled the beans. "This mean girl at school called me a dirty blonde," I choked out.

"Aw, honey. But you don't need to—"

"Please?" I asked. Begged. The look in my eyes must have convinced her, because she rung up my purchase and took my money. I triumphantly collected my bag and my change, then slipped out of the store.

I shoved the bag into my backpack and hurried home. I didn't want to get there too late, since walking too slowly was also on the list of things that made my dad mad at me.

Chapter 35
Hair Dye

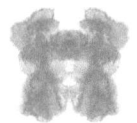

That night, I carefully opened the box and read the instructions. It recommended doing some sort of "test piece" of hair to check for allergies. I didn't want to waste the box, because I wasn't sure what would happen if I mixed it all together and then didn't use it. I only had four dollars left after buying candy and hair dye; it would take another week of skipping school lunch to save up enough for another box.

Another week of being a dirty blonde.

I stared at my reflection in the mirror. Did my hair have a greenish tint, after being in that place all summer? The strands did look darker, sadder. Like I'd had my whole childhood ripped away while I'd been in that windowless Isolation room.

Instead of doing the allergy test, I put on the plastic pair of gloves and mixed the bottles of chemicals together. I read the directions two more times, then began lathering up the roots of my hair. I worked the ammonia-smelling cream through each long strand of hair, until everything was wet and smelly.

I waited in the bathroom for the full thirty minutes, then rinsed the dye out of my hair. After I finished showering, I stared in the mirror at the final result.

I'd gone blonde, alright. Platinum blonde.

I wasn't sure what my dad would say. Would he yell at me? Would he send me back? Surely he'd ask where I'd found the money to buy it.

Maybe I'd lie and say my mom gave me some money. He probably wouldn't call her. And I had gotten to see her the other day.

She'd stood next to me like she'd wanted to hug me. But we weren't like that. She didn't hug, and I didn't ask for things she couldn't give me. I knew she wasn't well, and I'd accepted her for who she was.

But I also knew I wasn't like her.

I stared at my reflection, thinking about that stupid song again.

Man in the Mirror. No. I was staring at the eleven-year-old suddenly platinum blonde girl in the mirror.

At least if I was going to get sent away again, I would have earned it. I'd wiped away every inch of dirty blonde in my hair and done everything I could think of to hide who I really was.

I didn't want anyone to see the filth of lying on that Isolation room floor, the straight jacket wrapped around me as I tried to dodge my own vomit, the times I'd cried, and no one had come to rescue me.

"I'm asking her to change her ways," I whispered softly into the mirror just as my brother knocked on the door.

"Are you almost done?" Nick demanded.

"Um, yeah. Sorry!" I said.

I quickly buried the hair dye box in the trash and wrapped a towel around my head like they did in those television shows. I knew Nick would rat me out in an instant, and I needed to try to hide what I'd done for a little longer.

I didn't want to go back to the hospital yet.

But Nick didn't notice.

My dad didn't notice.

Not even my nosy stepmom noticed. It took a week before she glanced up at me over dinner and said, "Did you color your hair?"

I shrugged, not answering. Instead, I asked to be excused and went back to my room.

Chapter 36
Family Time

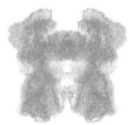

More than anything, I wanted to go back to whatever it felt like before I'd wasted away all summer in the hospital. I was already changing; I felt like there was a dark stain that marked me. Everybody could probably tell something was wrong with me just by glancing in my direction.

I would have given anything, even my favorite stuffed animal, to just feel like a normal kid again. To have some sort of family activity that made me feel like I was still part of this family. To play video games with Nick like we used to.

My dad used to take us to watch midnight trains as they moved through our city. He was always counting the engines and cars as they passed us by. He used to tell stories about trains he'd seen. I remembered going to the train museum up north with him, and I wanted that more than anything. Maybe he would like me again if I studied about railroads and train cars. Maybe he wouldn't look at me like he wanted to send me away.

Those were the thoughts swirling in my head when I woke up that Saturday morning. I hurried downstairs to get a bowl of cereal, wondering if my dad would still be eating breakfast. He always spent more time reading the newspaper on the weekends, and he had a predictable routine.

Sure enough, when I sat down at the table with my box of cereal, my dad had his chair at the end. He was already deep into the sports section. I had to figure out how to get his attention before he got to the comics. That was always where he stopped.

I poured the sugary circles into my bowl, watching the rainbow of colors land at odd patterns. Then, I carefully added milk, making sure I didn't spill. He usually got upset if I spilled milk.

When I capped the milk and deposited it back in the fridge, I heard my dad standing up in the next room. I hurried back to the dining room table, trying not to look like I was rushing. The last thing I needed was for him to wonder if I was up to something. All I was up to was trying to not get sent away again. It was the underlying tension that I carried with me every moment of every day.

A quick glance at the folded newspaper on the table told me he had reached the comics page in record speed. The black and white cartoons were only two pages on every day of the week except for Sundays, when they were an entire colorful section of their own. Had he really had time to read them? Or was he hurrying away again, avoiding me?

I felt like he didn't want to be around me at all. Like something was wrong with me.

"Dad, I was thinking," I started. He didn't look up, just continued gathering his bowl and box of cereal. "How about we go for a bike ride? I can pack sandwiches."

He shook his head. "No. We're going on a car ride today."

"Oh." I sat down, the energy deflating right out of me like I was a balloon with a large hole in its side. I sunk my spoon into the bowl, ready to just get it over with. There was no joy in sugary loops of cereal if I had to deal with my stepmom on a car ride. She always had something to complain about. "Where are we going?"

"Just for a drive. Terri's going to stay here. She has a headache."

That got my attention. I glanced up at my dad, but he still wasn't looking at me. "Okay. Is Nick coming, too?" I tried not to sound too happy, but the joy was infused with each word. No Terri!

"He's already ready. We're just waiting for you."

I nodded. A car ride with Nick and my dad! And my stepmom was staying behind. It was almost like we would get to have fun again.

"Don't forget to take your medicine." My orange pill was waiting in the center of the table, next to the napkin holder, atop a folded napkin. Great.

I muttered something that probably sounded like agreement. Sure, I would toss today's orange pill somewhere. There was no way I was taking any more drugs, though.

All I had to do was eat and get ready. I couldn't wait to go on an adventure.

Chapter 37
Group Home

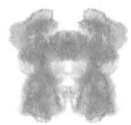

The road trip started out like any other drive. My dad and Nick hopped in the front of the van, since Nick had called shotgun way before I even knew we were going. I hopped into the back seat, content to just be in the same vehicle with them. My dad even had his Tupperware container of chips in the car, like when we went on long road trips. He was always prepared so that we never had to stop for snacks.

"Where are we going?" I asked as the van merged into traffic on the I-85 north. This part of the highway could lead to many places. At least we weren't headed towards the hospital, which was a huge relief. I hadn't come up with an escape plan if that happened again, but I was determined not to go back there.

"You'll see," my dad said, turning the radio volume up just a little louder. He had the Oldies station on, and every so often he bellowed out a song. Nick chatted with him quietly, mostly about classwork at junior high.

We passed by Charlotte, then continued north. Maybe we were going to the train museum? Could it be? That was an hour north, all the way up in Spencer. The museum was right next to the highway, and we got to exit on the left side of the interstate. I loved that weird side exit, then the short trek to a large brick building that looked like it should be a warehouse. Inside, there were automobiles from the 1950s, and there was a real train there, too. We had gone on it for a short train ride once, and even though it only went a short distance, it was cool to get on there and travel to the end of the track, then watch as the engineer maneuvered the train on a turnabout until we went back in the other direction.

But we didn't go to Spencer. I watched as we passed the left exit, and dad kept driving. "Are we going to see Melinda?" I asked. She was all the way in Virginia Tech by then, and that was a long drive. That would have surprised me, but my dad didn't answer. He just kept talking to Nick, like I wasn't even there.

I eventually got tired and rested my head against the window. My vision had been unfocused since getting out of the hospital, and I was going to have to get my eyes checked pretty soon. I didn't want to ask for glasses, and I was kind of mad about it. I was certain of why my vision had changed, and I blamed him for all of it.

My dad pulled off the interstate, his demeanor suddenly changed. He turned off the radio and glared at me in the rearview mirror. Nick clammed up. I watched him for clues. Did he know what was happening?

He drove a few miles before pulling off the main road onto a tree-lined street. He reached a long, brick building that looked like an office building, then parked the van.

"Get out," he said to me.

I unbuckled my seat belt, that bad feeling I had gotten in therapy circle rolling through me again.

When I was standing up next to the van, my dad approached. "Do you see this building?" he asked. I nodded. "This is the group home where I sent Kevin."

I squinted, noticing how someone was lifting up a corner of the blinds in one of the rooms. It wasn't an office at all. It was another kid prison. A place for problem children. A place where parents sent their unwanted kids and locked
them away.

"If you don't behave, I'll send you here."

I wanted to know what I'd done that was so awful. He hadn't yelled at me about the pills. I'd gone to therapy. I hadn't missed any school. I'd turned in all my homework.

But I wasn't brave anymore. I didn't want to fight with him. It was too soon. He would just send me away again.

I had argued with Terri a few days earlier. Was that what had set him off?

I glanced over at him. His jaw was set. He was staring at the building with anger, while all I felt was fear. The feeling of being unwanted. Even with non-dirty blonde hair. Even with good grades and better behavior. No matter what I did, I suddenly understood it would never be enough.

"You see that lawn?" he continued. "The kids cut the grass. They do all the chores. They keep this place spotless."

He was promising me the same fate as my brother, and I had no clue where my brother had ended up. He'd been sent away and stayed gone.

He'd been taken from me.

Was that what he wanted? He wanted to send me away from my family, too?

"I'll be good," I whispered.

Maybe. I couldn't promise to be better than him. He wasn't behaving. Why did I have to act better than a grown adult? Why was he being so mean?

I wasn't sure. But I knew I needed to come up with a better plan. I didn't want to go to a random group home.

I stared out the window for the long ride home, watching as we passed by towns that I'd never paid attention to before. Now, though, I knew that some of the kids I'd met over the summer lived in each of these towns. And I knew that group homes were hidden in plain sight.

If he was going to send me away again, I wouldn't let him send me back to the hospital or that hideous group home. There had to be a better way.

Chapter 38
Boarding School Book

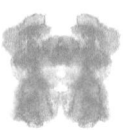

I locked myself in my room upstairs, grateful for a chance to hide. The ever-looming threat of "going back" to the Seventh Floor kept me focused on getting away. There was no way I would ever let my dad force me to go there again. I just didn't know how I was going to accomplish such a wild goal.

And now, there was the newest threat. He was thinking about sending me to a group home!

Fortunately, my dad was preoccupied with my stepmom's constant drama. She'd been more irritable at dinner that night, and she'd shouted at me when I didn't want to eat. Then, she'd started to cry.

"Eat your food! Can't you see you're making your stepmom depressed?"

I didn't care. She'd dropped enough blame on me for a lifetime, and I was unaffected by her tears. She knew how to bring on the waterworks at a moment's notice, always pointing to me as the instigator. Even when I'd done nothing more than push my food around my plate with my fork.

My dad glared at me for the rest of dinner, which ended abruptly when Terri stormed out of the room. Shortly after I'd dumped my food in my dog's bowl outside, my dad was climbing into his car with Terri.

She had a suitcase with her, which could only mean one of two things.

Either she was going to go stay with her mother or she was on her way back to the Seventh Floor. Either one would have made me happy. Her presence was like a dark cloud that hovered over the house at all times.

I was grateful when they drove away. I knew that if he tried another family meeting stunt, I'd never set foot in that hospital again. There was no way I'd go back. He probably knew that, which is why he'd tricked me into going on that stupid car ride to see the place where he'd abandoned my brother all those years earlier.

While my dad was gone, I considered running away. I didn't have enough money saved yet, so I tried to distract myself. I needed to stay calm.

I flipped through a teen magazine I'd bought. At the back, I saw an ad that suddenly filled me with hope.

There was a tiny box shaped ad with a one eight hundred number that I could call to request a "free" boarding school guide. It had the names and locations of all the schools in the country, and it promised to talk about financial aid and activities.

Maybe that was what I needed. My dad was obviously willing to dump his money into hospital copays. What if I could convince him to send me away to a decent place, instead? A place where I could just read, a place where I wasn't locked away for refusing to take meds I didn't even need. A place where I could finally be a kid again.

I picked up the phone and called the number. The book would arrive in just a few days.

That was enough to distract me from whatever had happened to Terri.

Chapter 39
TTI Brochures

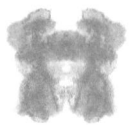

I hadn't been in my dad's room much since I'd gotten out of the hospital. When Terri was home, I was forbidden from getting near them. But now, she was back in the Seventh Floor. I nervously stepped into his room, bracing myself for whatever would happen next.

My dad was sitting in his rocking chair, which he'd propped up beside his bed. He had a full deck of cards splayed out on his blanket, playing solitaire against the dim light from a nearby lamp. His room looked mostly the way I'd remembered it, except there were a few more doilies and Southern style arts and crafts that made it clear that Terri had been there.

"Dad," I said. I was holding the boarding school booklet in my hand, and I'd dog-eared all the programs that said things like "scholarships" or "low tuition." He didn't want me there, and I didn't want to stay.

He glanced up, a strange look on his face. "Oh. I thought I locked the door."

I wasn't sure why he was trying so hard to keep me out. Before being hospitalized, the most I'd ever done was pocket a few dimes from his coin jar. The really tasty chocolate chip cookies at school called out to me sometimes, and everyone wanted to get a treat sometimes.

Especially me, after spending a summer eating stale hospital food and canned fruit.

I glanced over at his dresser, noticing the brochures. There were a half dozen pamphlets for wilderness camps and programs for bad kids. Phrases like the ones Charter Pines used on their television commercials for hospitals were written across the front pages of each brochure: "Warning signs" and "Are you worried about your teen?" in bright red or yellow letters.

At eleven, I wasn't a teen. I was an Adolescent. A kid who didn't belong anywhere. I most certainly didn't fit in here anymore, and I knew that my dad was trying to figure out where to send me.

"I got this really cool book in the mail," I said, showing him the front cover of my boarding school guide. "It has info on all the boarding schools around here, and I was-"

"We can't afford that," he interrupted.

I'd done the math. I knew that one year in boarding school wasn't even a fraction of the amount he'd been spending on the hospital. But... "But you can afford the hospital?" I demanded, clutching the book against my chest. "You don't even want me here." It was true; there was no denying it. The random car ride to Kevin's old group home had made that perfectly clear, even though I'd already figured it out during my time on the Seventh Floor.

He stared at me, like he was looking right through me. His uncaring dark eyes didn't truly see me, his broken-hearted little girl who was terrified of being locked up again. If he was going to send me away anyway, why couldn't it at least be on my own terms? Why didn't I have any say at all in where I lived or whether or not I had to take those stupid pills?

I studied the bookshelf that stood against his wall. It was where he'd kept his old chemistry books from college. The titles were blurry now. I used to be able to read them. Even that infuriated me. I used to be able to see much better, before they'd drugged me all summer. Since returning home, I hadn't taken a single pill, but my vision hadn't improved at all.

"I don't need this right now," he grumbled, turning back to his cards.

There was no point sticking around. I spun around and hurried out of the room that I used to feel comfortable visiting, but now felt like a foreign place. I was beyond ready to retreat to the safety of my own bedroom. Just as I was about to walk out, I skidded to a halt. My eyes lingered on a logo I recognized from tv.

I took two steps back towards my dad's dresser. I picked up a brochure and traced the words with my fingers. It said things like: "Residential treatment centers" and "Wilderness camp."

"Are you going to send me away?" I asked as I picked up one of the flyers. "These cost a lot of money. Why won't you just send me to a nice school? I'll study hard, and you won't have to deal with me!"

"No."

"I don't understand," I pleaded. "The hospital didn't make me into a perfect kid. These won't, either. Can't you just send me somewhere I want to go?"

"No," he repeated.

"Can I go live with my mom?"

He looked up, our eyes meeting. A chill ran down my spine. "You know why you can't do that."

I did, I really did. But she was so much kinder than him. And I wanted someone to want me. Around here, I was
always in the way. "Dad, are you going to send me away?"

He shrugged. "I haven't decided."

I picked up another brochure. It was for the group home we had visited. "Why? What's so wrong with me? I wasn't like any of those kids in the hospital!"

"We're not going to talk about this."

"But I wasn't. Dad, I don't drink or smoke. I don't do drugs. I'm not a bad kid."

There was a moment, a split second when I felt like he was going to change his mind. When I stared into his eyes and felt like he was hearing me. But then he lowered his head again and began to pick up the cards. The clock by his bed said 8:05.

"Look, I'm tired. Just go to bed."

"Dad, please don't do this!" I begged again.

"I'm done talking about this." His voice was stern, and part of me recoiled at the sound. A memory flashed through my head, reminding me how he stood silently while the men grabbed me at the hospital.

And he was done discussing wilderness camps and placements. He stared at his hands or his bed or something else, but not at me. He stopped talking to me completely, his hands going through the motions of shuffling the deck of cards and laying them out again. He had time for another game of Solitaire, but he wasn't willing to have this conversation with me.

"Dad," I whispered, my voice cracking. "I'll be good."

I dropped the brochures and the book on his dresser, then hurried out of the room. I raced up the stairs two at a time, my eyes beginning to fill with tears that I wouldn't let myself cry. I made it to my room, where I bolted the door shut.

"What will I do, what will I do?" I muttered to myself, pacing around the room. I needed to get out of there before my dad did whatever he was planning. I needed to get away. But where? And how?

If only I had one of the older kids' numbers from the hospital. They would have known what to do.

Chapter 40
Escape

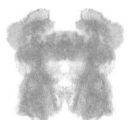

I'd been back at my dad's house for almost a month. Terri was still in the hospital. And each day, I'd saved up a dollar instead of buying lunch. I sat on my bed, counting the money. Wondering.

Would it be enough to get away? I didn't know where I'd go. Maybe to the beach?

What would I need? A tent? Camping supplies? A guard dog? My neighbors had cute Doberman puppies that they didn't seem too interested in; they'd ignored the entire last litter, and none had survived. Maybe I'd pack up all my stuff in a big backpack and take a puppy with me. I could start my life over again, with the waves crashing on a nearby beach while I roasted marshmallows over an open fire. Even though I'd never been camping, and I didn't know how to start a fire. Would the tent come with instructions? I'd seen people struggling with building them on a few tv shows.

A knock at the door startled me. I quickly tried to stuff the wad of bills into my pocket, but Nick entered fast enough that he was able to see them.

"I've been saving up, too," he said.

Our eyes met. Why? He didn't need to leave. My dad treasured him. He was the perfect kid. Great grades, never talked back. Wore socks. He wasn't a problem child like me.

"How?" I asked, avoiding the obvious.

He sat down on the edge of my bed, a grin forming. "It's easy. I bought some bubble gum packs, and I sell each piece of gum for a quarter."

Gum cost a quarter a pack back then, for five pieces. So he was making a dollar off of each pack.

Nick didn't ask how I'd collected my stack of dollar bills. And I wasn't about to tell him.

"What are you saving for?"

"Mario Brothers. Do you want to split the cost?"

I smiled. I'd been wanting to play that game for more than the ten-minute sample we could play at the nearby toy store. "That would be cool. I've got twenty-seven dollars." I'd even pulled money from my plastic piggy bank.

"Me too." He was genuinely smiling. We hadn't had a happy moment in a while, at least, not together.

"What will we tell dad when he asks how we bought it?" I asked.

We both sat there for a few minutes, thinking of ideas. Our dad would ask. He always asked. It wasn't like he knew Nick was selling gum or I was skipping lunch to pocket the dollar bill every day. But he would… know. And even if both of us were involved, I would take the fall. It was the way things were.

I didn't want to go back to the hospital.

The beach sounded cool, but I was eleven. How was I supposed to survive on twenty dollars?

There had to be a way. Finally, I spoke. "Maybe we could say Mom bought it for us."

Nick nodded. "That's actually a great idea."

"It's not like Dad would ask her. They don't even talk."

"Then let's go to the store. We've got two hours till Dad gets home."

I hopped up, grateful for an excuse to get out of the house. With Nick, I was safe. Terri didn't complain if I was hanging out with him. It was when I walked home alone that she became outraged. Or when I took a bike ride all by myself. Even though we'd been free range kids since our mom had left a few years earlier.

The walk to the store was short, since we lived right next to the strip mall. Nick proudly walked up to the salesman and told him that we were buying Mario Brothers 3. The new one. It had been out for two years, and we'd been dreaming of owning it for so long. The sample only let us play the first few episodes, but we didn't know what came after that. I wanted to explore each kingdom and beat Bowser. Besides, Nick had beaten Zelda without me when I'd been sent away for the summer, and I just didn't want to play that game anymore. It reminded me of the time I'd lost.

The salesman shrugged and got the game for us, then handed it to Nick at the register. We pulled out our wads of dollar bills and coins. It turned out Nick mostly had quarters, which made sense because he was in the quarter business. Our money was messy and heavy, but it was enough. We were finally buying the game we'd been dreaming about.

After the cashier counted our money, we were given the coveted game. Our prize.

Outside of the store, Nick tossed the receipt and bag in the trash. "No evidence." He unwrapped the plastic covering so there wouldn't be any clues.

"Right," I said. Nick was so much smarter than me. I wondered if I'd learn to be like him when I was twelve.

We couldn't wait to get home to play our new game; Nick started running first and I trailed after him. Maybe I'd be saving up to escape my dad's house soon, but I was still eleven. And video games were another form of escape. After all, I could always skip a few dozen more lunches if I had to, stashing those dollar bills for a rainy day. But on that cool day in September, we were about to defeat our first castle from the evil villain and save the princess. Deep down, I knew I would do whatever it took to stay out of the Seventh Floor.

The summer had changed me; I wasn't naïve about the world anymore. I wasn't afraid. No; I was angry. And I knew that I would have to get out before he dumped me someplace far worse than Seventh Floor. My imagination wasn't advanced enough to know what he was capable of, but I kept picturing that group home where he'd abandoned Kevin.

I would choose where I would go. I would find safety, one way or another. I just didn't know how to find it or where to look. It was hard being eleven.

But I couldn't save myself yet. At least I could practice on a computer, fighting against a monster who kept trapping a young girl in places she didn't belong. And that would have to be enough for me.

Author's Note

When I was being interviewed about my memoir, Hindsight: Coming of Age on the Streets of Hollywood, one of the interviewers asked me a remarkable question. He asked, "If someone had been able to intervene and help prevent all the things you went through, at what age should they have done that?"

My answer was 11. At 11 years old, I was already marked by trauma, but those traumas were recoverable. My parents had gotten divorced. My mom had mental illness. A sibling was in foster care. I had a new stepmom. All of those things were challenging, but they weren't nearly at the level of trauma that my dad and his new wife managed to throw at me from 11 and beyond.

I needed books that helped me understand my experience. I needed adults who were paying attention, asking the right questions. I needed safeguards. I found none of those things.

What I found instead was a Pandora's Box of bad ideas. The kids on the adolescent ward taught me things I hadn't known. How to run away. How to escape. They told me about foster care, that place my brother had been sent away to.

And after getting out, I had one goal. I vowed to never get locked in a little room again and lose my freedom. I would fail miserably a few years later, but at least I knew what I needed to feel safe. And I would spend the next seven or eight years fighting for it.

I ended up on the streets of Hollywood at 16, years after this incident. By then, I'd lost all trust in adults and refused to go into any program that might or might not have helped me. Had those early experiences been different, I may have been more willing to trust the adults around me and consider a placement. But my trust had been broken, and I'd been abused at the hands of the people that should have been protecting me.

When I was finally off the streets and more stable, at 19, I called the hospital where I'd been at 11 to request my records. I was starting to understand just how severe that early inpatient hospitalization had been, and how much it had thrown my life off course. But over seven years had passed since I'd been hospitalized, and the person who answered the phone told me the records had been destroyed "because [they] only had to hold them for 7 years." I was devastated; I'd wanted answers, but they'd covered their tracks. I had no proof of what they'd done to me. Of the times they'd terrorized me. And my own family had gaslit me for years. Nobody understood how much that summer had shifted my life off course.

That's why this book is so important. I want young readers to know that they absolutely can DEMAND safety. Demand protection. None of us deserve to be abused. There is always a way to fight back. Nursing boards. Medical boards. Hospital administrators. Child protective services. The police. Any of those people could have and should have intervened. Because it wasn't just me. There was always a kid in Isolation.

I was 11. I never should have been there. I still can't verbalize what I did that was so bad to deserve 2 months and 10 days of hospitalization. I never should have been forced to take medications, especially under duress. Locked in Isolation, deprived of regular meals, a bathroom. It was inhumane.

We need to speak up and speak out against mistreatment of kids. And we need to create a safe space for young people. There are resources listed on the next page. Reach out to the trusted hotline phone numbers and resource groups if you are in danger or need someone to step in to make sure your needs are met. You deserve to be loved, to feel safe, and to make decisions about what you put into your own body.

Thank you for reading. I appreciate all of you so much.

Sheryl
(I gave up the nickname Sheri when I was 17.)
Survivor of TTI inpatient hospitalization, 1990

Reading Group Questions

1. What early traumas did Sheri reveal when she started thinking about her mom and siblings?
2. Why did Sheri think she was being kidnapped at the family meeting?
3. What types of behaviors got Sheri placed in Isolation?
4. What was Sheri afraid of?
5. At the end of the book, Sheri vows to escape. The next book chronicles how she escapes and the consequences of running away. What other options did Sheri have?
6. If this story occurred now, what could Sheri do differently to stay safe?
7. Sheri is now an adult and does not have a psychiatric diagnosis. She is a mom of three adult children, married, and is a physician. What does this imply about the diagnosis of bipolar disorder that the psychiatrist gave her when she was initially hospitalized?
8. There is an entire industry that is called the **Troubled Teen Industry**, made up of similarly abusive programs that force young people to take medications and use punishments and isolation for "therapy." Based on this story, what protections do you think need to be created to make sure kids in any form of treatment are kept safe?

The Hindsight Junior Series

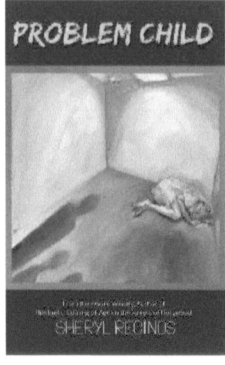  

Join Sheri as she fights to survive her adolescent years.

Book 1: Problem Child

Eleven-year-old Sheri has been looking forward to summer all year. She will finally get to play unlimited video games and binge read at the local library. Except… her dad has a different idea.

After a "family meeting" on the psych unit for her new stepmom, Sheri's dad decides to leave her on the adolescent ward. She's terrified and at first, thinks she has been kidnapped.

Book 2: Pink Stars

Thirteen-year-old Sheri gave herself TWO choices. Escape by suicide or by running away. Desperate to stay alive, Sheri steals $250 from her dad and buys a one-way bus ticket to Los Angeles.

Soon, she's arrested for being a runaway, Sheri finds herself in the foster care system and keeps running. Will she ever feel safe enough to stay in one place?

Book 3: Lil Hollywood

Sheri is terrified. She stole money from her dad when she ran away from home a few months ago, and he pressed charges!

The judge sentenced to TWO YEARS in maximum security juvenile prison. Maximum security is the one place she can't run away from. Or can she?

Resources

If there's someone who makes you feel unsafe, please find a trusted adult that you can talk to. Great examples include your parents, siblings, teachers, and school counselor.

Consider the following emergency numbers:

Crisis Lines:
- Suicide Hotline 800-273-8255
- Trevor Project (Suicide Prevention for LGBTQ youth) 866-488-7386
- Crisis Text Line 741-741
- National Child Abuse Hotline 800-4-A-CHILD or Text CHILDHELP to 847411

For homeless or runaway teens:
- Covenant House Nineline 800-999-9999
- National Runaway Switchboard 800-RUNAWAY
- Boys Town National Hotline (helps Boys & Girls) 800 448-3000

Spotlight on My Friend's Place

What is My Friend's Place?

My Friend's Place is a program located in Hollywood, California that works with young people and youths experiencing homelessness. They work with young people ages 12 to 30, and their children.

The Safe Haven Program focuses on immediate needs of young people, such as food, clothing, showers, transportation, and communication. They serve over 700 youths per year, provide almost 16,000 meals, over 1300 showers, and link young people to emergency housing. The Intake and Crisis Care team helps make sure young people have access to identification and helps with case management services.

The Transformative Education Program gives young people opportunities to be creative, learn new skills, and begin the pathway towards self-sufficiency.

They have creative arts workshops, such as creative writing, fashion design, circus arts, vocal coaching, songwriting and music recording, digital media, and visual arts activities. Young people in these workshops often find new ways to express themselves, discover new talents, and build rapport with staff.

The Health and Well Being Program helps connect young people to health and wellness services, provides case management for immediate needs and to begin applying for supportive housing, and offers a Parenting program for young people who are pregnant or parenting.

Bookmarks made by young people for the Corner Collective, on sale at the L.A. Times Festival of Books. (The young people earn money for their artwork.)

How can I help?

My Friend's Place is a nonprofit organization that provides free services for young people. Check out their website at www.myfriendsplace.org for more information about the many ways you can get involved.

MFP is primarily supported by donations and would love your support. They always appreciate focused gift drives, such as backpack, blankets, sleeping bags, clothing and hygiene supplies, and holiday gifts. There is a monthly wishlist on their website with their most updated needs.

Local groups can volunteer to bring a special meal and serve it to young people. They can volunteer to help onsite, such as organizing donations or teaching a class. Additionally, there is a young professionals group called the Emerging Leaders Council, made up of community members who are excited about fundraising, volunteering with youth, and organizing social events for people to learn more about how to help end youth homelessness.

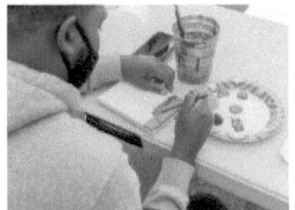  

From the author:

Why do I love My Friend's Place?

This program was instrumental in helping me get off the streets as a teen. I know their low-barrier, trauma-informed approach works, because it worked for me and many other young people I knew.

At first, I only went to the program for help with my basic needs, like food and clothing. Over time, I started to trust the staff more, and eventually I was able to ask for what I really needed.

My case manager helped me come up with a plan to get off the streets and connected me with parenting resources when I had my first child. I started volunteering with them after I graduated from college, and recently became the first alumni member on the Board of Directors.

I can't wait to see a future where we're all success stories because we end youth homelessness. For now, let's make a difference in the lives of young people.

Serving meals for young people. The author's husband and son helped out for this holiday feast.

Los Angeles Marathon team t-shirt, 2022.

About the Author

Sheryl Recinos is a mom, physician, and writer. She lives in Los Angeles with her husband and adult children. They have a "zoo" of rescued pets: 3 dogs, 2 cats, turtles, tortoises, fish, and even a snake named Tomato.

When she released her first book **Hindsight: Coming of Age on the Streets of Hollywood** in 2018, she realized that she had been looking for stories like this one her whole life. She wants to help young people find their own voices. Her greatest dream is that all young people will find safety and housing.

www.ingramcontent.com/pod-product-compliance
Ingram Content Group UK Ltd.
Pitfield, Milton Keynes, MK11 3LW, UK
UKHW041428180426